Read Well Science Digest: Where in the World?

Teacher's Guide

Unit 23

Review

Note: See New and Important Objectives on page 2 for a complete list of skills taught and reviewed.

Critical Foundations in Primary Reading

Marilyn Sprick, Ann Watanabe, Karen Akiyama-Paik, and Shelley V. Jones

Sopris West®
EDUCATIONAL SERVICES

A Cambium Learning® Company

BOSTON, MA • LONGMONT, CO

ISBN 13-digit: 978-1-60218-546-3
ISBN 10-digit: 1-60218-546-8

7 8 9 10 11 B&B 16 15 14 13 12
167062/6-12

Table of Contents
Unit 23
Read Well Science Digest
Where in the World?

Table of Contents

Table of Contents

23

READ WELL Plus

Science Digest

SCIENCE & LITERATURE
FOR KIDS

An animal that **walks 125 miles** to lay an egg

Where in the world?

A clever cat that teases **fish**

A desert made of . . . **ice?**

Sopris West

Letter Sounds and Combinations

Cumulative Review of *Read Well 1* Sounds and Combinations (Ss, Ee, ee, Mm, Aa, Dd, th, Nn, Tt, Ww, Ii, Th, Hh, Cc, Rr, ea, sh, Sh, Kk, -ck, oo, ar, wh, Wh, ĕ, -y as in fly, Ll, Oo, Bb, all, Gg, Ff, Uu, er, oo as in book, Yy, a schwa, Pp, ay, Vv, Qq, Jj, Xx, or, Zz, a_e, -y as in baby, i_e, ou, ow as in cow, ch, Ch, ai, igh, o_e, ir) and:

Unit 2	Unit 3		Unit 5	Unit 6
aw /aw/ **Paw** Voiced	**ew** /ōō/ **Crew** Voiced	**ue** /ōō/ **Blue** Voiced	**u_e** /ōō/ **Flute** Bossy E Voiced	**ow** /ōōō/ **Snow** Voiced (Long)	**ge** /j/ **Page** Voiced

Unit 6	Unit 7		Unit 8		Unit 10
-dge /j/ **Badge** Voiced	**ci** /sss/ **Circle** Unvoiced	**ce** /sss/ **Center** Unvoiced	**kn** /nnn/ **Knee** Voiced	**ph** /fff/ **Phone** Unvoiced	**oa** /ōōō/ **Boat** Voiced (Long)

Unit 11		Unit 12		Unit 13
oi /oi/ **Point** Voiced	**ea** /ĕĕĕ/ **Bread** Voiced (Short)	**gi** /j/ **Giraffe** Voiced	**au** /au/ **Astronaut** Voiced	**oy** /oy/ **Boy** Voiced

Affixes (including morphographs—affixes taught with meaning) and Open Syllables

Cumulative Review of *Read Well 1* Affixes (-ed, -en, -es, -ing, -ly, -s, -y, -tion) and:

Unit 2	Unit 3		Unit 5		Unit 6
re- Means again as in reread	**un-** Means not as in unhappy	**ex-** as in excited	**o** Open syllable /ō/ as in open and moment	**-ful** Means full of as in colorful	**bi-** Means two as in bicycle

Unit 7	Unit 8	Unit 11	Unit 12	Unit 13	
de- as in detective	**-able** as in comfortable	**i** Open syllable /ī/ as in silence and pilot	**be-** as in before	**-ous** as in enormous	**dis-** as in discover

Unit 14		Unit 15		Unit 16	
-al as in animal	**-ible** as in flexible	**-or** Means one who as in actor	**-ment** as in apartment	**-ic** as in scientific	**pre-** Means before as in preview

Unit 17		Unit 18		Unit 19	
-ity as in activity	**-sion** as in permission	**-ness** as in fairness	**-less** Means without as in helpless	**in-** as in insert	**im-** Means not as in impossible

Introduction
Read Well Science Digest: Where in the World?

Story Notes

The popular *Read Well Science Digest* magazine format resurfaces to introduce students to two extremely different parts of the world: the lush tropical rain forest and the inhospitable continent of Antarctica.

Antarctica: Introduce students to the coldest, driest, and windiest place on Earth.
What's Black and White and Royalty? The emperor penguin, of course. Students will be fascinated by how penguins have adapted to their harsh environment.
A Penguin's Calendar: It's a year in the life of everyone's favorite flightless bird.
Thor, Emily, and the Little Successor: Students continue to learn facts about penguins in this fictional account of a young penguin's first trek back to his birthplace.
Tropical Rain Forest: Students switch gears from the driest place on Earth to the wettest— the tropical rain forest. Along the way, they meet jaguars, howler monkeys, and harpy eagles.
Miss Tam's Corner: The well-traveled librarian makes a guest appearance to pass along tips to help take care of our planet.

> **CAUTION**
> **(Reminder)**
> Do not read the Read Aloud recommendations during small group instruction. Reserve this time for students to read.

Recommended Read Alouds

The *Read Well 2* suggested read alouds enhance small group instruction—providing opportunities to further build background knowledge and vocabulary.

Penguin Chick by Betty Tatham
Nonfiction • Science

Ever wonder how baby penguins are born? This fun, fact-filled book describes the incredible lengths an emperor penguin goes to in order to have a baby.

The Last Badge by George McClements
Fiction • Narrative

Grizzly Scout Sam needs to earn his Moon Frog badge. The problem is that the Moon Frog hibernates for 30 years, emerging only on the 12th hour of the 10th night of the 8th month. Sam learns valuable lessons about wildlife during his quest to find the frog.

Read Well Connections
Penguin Chick adds to the penguin facts students learn in the *Read Well Science Digest*. *The Last Badge* raises good questions about the impact of human behavior on animals in the wild.

New and Important Objectives
A Research-Based Reading Program

Phonemic Awareness
Phonics
Fluency
Vocabulary
Comprehension

Phonics

Cumulative Letter Sounds and Combinations

Review • Ss, Ee, ee, Mm, Aa, Dd, th, Nn, Tt, Ww, Ii, Th, Hh, Cc, Rr, ea, sh, Sh, Kk, -ck, oo, ar, wh, Wh, ĕ, -y (as in fly), Ll, Oo, Bb, all, Gg, Ff, Uu, er, oo (as in book), Yy, a (schwa), Pp, ay, Vv, Qq, Jj, Xx, or, Zz, a_e, -y (as in baby), i_e, ou, ow (as in cow), ch, Ch, ai, igh, o_e, ir, aw, ew, ue, u_e, ow (as in snow), ge, -dge, ci, ce, kn, ph, oa, oi, ea (as in bread), gi, au, oy

Cumulative Affixes, Morphographs, and Open Syllables

Review • -ed, -en, -er, -es, -est, -ing, -ly, -s, -y, -tion, re-, un-, ex-, o (as in open), -ful, bi-, de-, -able, i (as in silence), be-, -ous, dis-, -al, -ible, -or, -ment, -ic, pre-, -ity, -sion, -ness, -less, in-, im-

★New Foreign Words

adiós, ciao, sayonara, sampai jumpa

★New Contractions

winter's

★New Proper Nouns

Antarctic, British Columbia, Costa Rica, Costa Rican, Emily's ◆ Finn, Finn's, Italian, Japanese, July, Natalie, Roland Tiensuu, Roland's, Sweden, Thor, Thor's, Vancouver

★New Pattern Words

bin ◆ bins, depths, dove, fir, freeze, freezing ◆ humph, keel, keeled, moist, prowl, prowls, shade ◆ sleds ◆ split ◆ sweep, trek, troop, troops, vines

*Known Pattern Words With Affixes • blasts, caring, checked, clicked, colder, coldest, creeps, cups, driest, dropping, ends, frog's, greeting, harsher, holds, howler, howls, joyous, jumps, males, marching, melts, moms, neared, nearer, nesting, perched, planning, presoak, proudly, reaches, reusable, roaring, sailing, shaving, storing, swiftly, swooshing, teases, wakes, wettest, wrapping

★New Compound and Hyphenated Words

birthdays, ever-watchful, farewell, humpback, never-ending, red-eyed, understory

---

* Known Pattern Words With Affixes, Known Tricky Words With Affixes, and **Known Multisyllabic Words With Affixes** have base words students have previously read. The words are new in this unit because they have not been previously read with the affix.

★ = New in this unit

◆ = Words that are not introduced in the exercises before they are read in the storybook

Phonics (continued)

★ **Other New Multisyllabic Words**

accomplishment, acre, acres, acrobat, agile, album, attract, attracts, blubber, calendar, canopy ◆ chilly, compost, composting, conserve, container, contributed, degree, degrees, disposable ◆ ducky, edit, editing, edition, emergent, environment, equator, eternal, feature, fluffy, flyer, flyers, folder, folders, grizzly, harpies, harpy, harpy's, huddle, huddled, hunker, hunkered, icy, instinct, landscape ◆ litter, magnificent, mantled, parade, parades, petrels, poster, preserve, rarely, razor, reduce, rookery, royalty, speckle, speckled, suction, talons, tapir, toboggan, tobogganed, tobogganing, tropical, trumpet, trumpeted, tuxedo

Known Multisyllabic Words With Affixes • collected, cookies, curiously, explorers, females, jaguar's, marvelous, penguin's, penguins, penguins', recognized, rediscovered, secretive, showers, silently, successors, surfaced, surroundings, televisions, temperatures, towels, turtles, umbrellas, uncomfortable, unprotected, valleys, windiest

★ **New Tricky Words**

leopards, lichens, precious, recycling, resources, species, toucan, zero

Known Tricky Words With Affixes • toward, warmest, warmth, water's, wears

Fluency

Accuracy, Expression, Phrasing, Rate

Vocabulary

New • Antarctic, Arctic, blizzard, composting, conserve, equator, eternal, exceptional, freezing, harsh, instinct, marvelous, rarely, reduce, reuse, strut, talons, temperature, territory, toboggan, trek

Review • Africa, algae, amazing, Australia, bellow, bittersweet, carnivore, community, continent, despite, dinosaur, ecosystem, embarrassed, emerge, emperor, endangered, energy, exhausted, fascinate, fossil, generation, habitat, hesitate, impressive, instinct, marvelous, ordinary, panic, perfect, pioneer, planet, predator, predator, prey, protect, prove, recognize, recycle, responsibility, splendid, successor, survive, talons, unique, unsettled, vast, wonderful

Reviewed in Context • adventure, Africa, algae, amazed, amazing, Australia, bellow, boast, brilliant, caption, carnivore, colony, community, confused, continent, creature, dangerous, decomposer, despite, determined, dinosaur, distressed, electricity, emerge, emperor, energy, eventful, expedition, fossil, generation, Ghana, habit, habitat, herbivore, hesitate, imagination, imagine, impressive, instinct, inventor, molt, natural, perfect, planet, practical, predator, prey, protect, protected, protection, prove, recognize, recycle, responsibility, roam, senses, shrug, splendid, successor, surface, survive, thrilled, towering, treasure, unique, unsettled, vacant, vast, volume, waste, wildlife

Idioms and Expressions

New • hunker down, keel over

Comprehension

Unit Genres
Nonfiction • Expository
Fiction • Narrative

Comprehension Processes
Build Knowledge: Factual, Procedural, Conceptual

	Day	1	2	3	4	5	6	7	8
Remember									
Defining									
Identifying (recalling)		S,C	S	S,C	E,S	S,C	S,C	S,C	C
Using									
Understand									
Defining (in your own words)		S		S	E,S,C	S		S	
Describing		S	S	S	S	S	S		
Explaining (rephrasing)			S	S	S		C		S
Illustrating							C		
Sequencing			C						
Summarizing		C	S	S		S	S	S	
Using		S,C	E,S,C	S	E,S,C	S	S	S,C	S
Visualizing			S						
Apply									
Demonstrating		S							
Explaining (unstated)		S	S	S	S		S	S	S,C
Illustrating					C			C	
Inferring		S	S	S,C	S	C	S	S	S,C
Making Connections (relating)			S	S		S			S
Predicting		S		S	S				
Using		S	S	S	S	S	S	S	
Analyze									
Classifying									
Comparing/Contrasting						S	S		
Distinguishing Cause/Effect									C
Drawing Conclusions		S	S	S	S	S	S		S,C
Inferring									
Evaluate									
Making Judgments									
Responding (personal)						S	C	C	C
Create									
Generating Ideas		S,C	E		C		C	C	C

E = Exercise, S = Storybook, C = Comprehension & Skill

Comprehension (continued)

Skills and Strategies

Day	1	2	3	4	5	6	7	8
Priming Background Knowledge								
Setting a Purpose for Reading	S	S	S	S		S		
Answering Questions	S	S	S	S	S	S	S	
Asking Questions								
Visualizing		S						
Comprehension Monitoring/Fix Ups								
Does it Make Sense?	C	C			C			
Looking Back								
Restating								
Summarizing								
Main Idea	C							
Retelling								
Supporting Details	C	S	S					
Understanding Text Structure								
Title, Author, Illustrator	S,C		S	S	S	S	S	
Fact or Fiction								
Genre (Classifying)			S					
Narrative								
Setting			S					
Main Character/Traits (Characterization)*			S					S
Goal								
Problem/Solution								
Action/Events/Sequence								
Outcome/Conclusion								
Lesson/Author's Message								
Expository								
Subject/Topic	S,C		C					
Heading								
Supporting Details (Facts/Information)	C	S	S,C	E	C	S,C		C
Main Idea	C		C					C
Using Graphic Organizers								
Chart					C			
Diagram (labeling)					C			
Hierarchy (topic/detail)	C		C					C
K-W-L								
Map (locating, labeling)					C			
Matrix (compare/contrast)								C
Sequence (linear, cycle, cause and effect)				C				
Story Map								
Web								

E = Exercise, S = Storybook, C = Comprehension & Skill

* Narrator

Comprehension (continued)

Study Skills

Day	1	2	3	4	5	6	7	8
Alphabetical Order								
Following Directions	C							
Locating Information	S,C			C	C			
Note Taking								
Previewing								
Reviewing		S	S	S		S		
Test Taking						C		C
Using Glossary	S		S	E,S	S		S	
Using Table of Contents	S,C							
Viewing	S	S		C	S	C		
Verifying					C			

Writing in Response to Reading

Day	1	2	3	4	5	6	7	8
Sentence Completion	C	C	C	C	C	C	C	
Making Lists					C			
Sentence Writing	C	C	C	C	C	C	C	C
Story Retell/Summary								
Fact Summary	C				C			
Paragraph Writing	C							
Report Writing								
Open-Ended Response					C	C		
Creative Writing	C				C	C		

Writing Traits

(Addressed within the context of Writing in Response to Reading)

Day	1	2	3	4	5	6	7	8
Ideas and Content								
Elaborating/Generating	C			C		C	C	C
Organization								
Introduction								
Topic Sentence	C					C		
Supporting Details	C					C		
Sequencing								
Word Choice								
Sophisticated Words (Tier 2 and 3)	C	C		C			C	C
Conventions								
Capital	C	C	C	C	C	C	C	C
Ending Punctuation	C	C	C	C	C	C	C	C
Other (commas, quotation marks)								
Presentation								
Handwriting	C	C	C	C	C	C	C	C
Neatness	C	C	C	C	C	C	C	C

E = Exercise, S = Storybook, C = Comprehension & Skill

Daily Lesson Planning

LESSON PLAN FORMAT

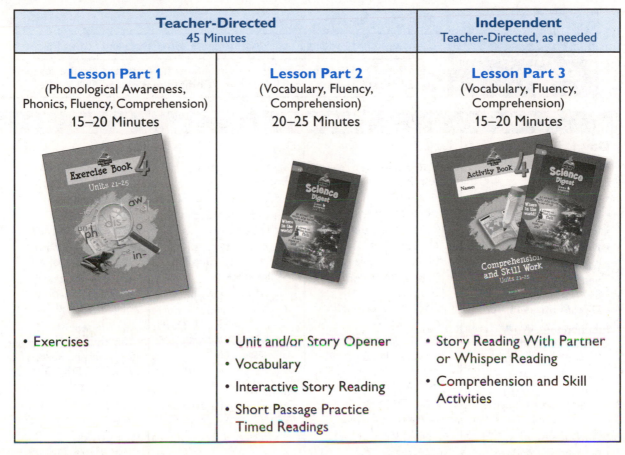

Teacher-Directed 45 Minutes		Independent Teacher-Directed, as needed
Lesson Part 1 (Phonological Awareness, Phonics, Fluency, Comprehension) 15–20 Minutes	**Lesson Part 2** (Vocabulary, Fluency, Comprehension) 20–25 Minutes	**Lesson Part 3** (Vocabulary, Fluency, Comprehension) 15–20 Minutes
• Exercises	• Unit and/or Story Opener • Vocabulary • Interactive Story Reading • Short Passage Practice Timed Readings	• Story Reading With Partner or Whisper Reading • Comprehension and Skill Activities

HOMEWORK

Read Well Homework (blackline masters of new *Read Well 2* passages) provides an opportunity for children to celebrate accomplishments with parents. Homework should be sent home on routine days.

ORAL READING FLUENCY ASSESSMENT

Upon completion of this unit, assess each student and proceed to Unit 24, as appropriate.

WRITTEN ASSESSMENT

During the time students would normally complete Comprehension and Skill Activities, students will be administered a Written Assessment that can be found on page 101 in the students' *Activity Book 4*.

Note: See Making Decisions for additional assessment information.

EXTENDING PLANS

Two plans illustrate how to use materials for students with various learning needs. As you set up your unit plan, always include *Read Well 2 Plus* Exercises and Story Reading on a daily basis. Unit 23 includes 8- and 10-Day Plans.

Plans	For groups that:
8-DAY	Complete Oral Reading Fluency Assessments with Passes and Strong Passes
10-DAY	Complete Oral Reading Fluency Assessments with Passes and require teacher-guided assistance with Story Reading and Comprehension and Skill Work

8-DAY PLAN

Day 1	Day 2	Day 3	Day 4
Teacher-Directed • Exercise 1 • Unit Opener • Letter From the Editor • Vocabulary Power! 1 • Antarctica! • Guide practice, as needed, on Comp & Skill 1 and Science Digest Entries 1a, 1b, 1c **Independent Work** • Repeated Reading: Partner or Whisper Read: Antarctica! • Comp & Skill 1 and Science Digest Entries 1a, 1b, 1c **Homework** • Homework Passage 1	**Teacher-Directed** • Exercise 2a • Exercise 2b: Focus Lesson • What's Black and White and Royalty? • A Penguin's Calendar • Guide practice on Comp & Skill 2 and Science Digest Entries 2a, 2b **Independent Work** • Repeated Reading: Partner or Whisper Read, What's Black and White and Royalty? • Comp & Skill 2 and Digest Entries 2a, 2b **Homework** • Homework Passage 2	**Teacher-Directed** • Exercise 3 • Vocabulary Power! 2 • Thor, Emily, and the Little Successor, Ch. 1 • Guide practice, as needed, on Comp & Skill 3 and 4 **Independent Work** • On Your Own: Partner or Whisper Read, Thor, Emily, and the Little Successor, Ch. 2 • Comp & Skill 3 and 4 **Homework** • Homework Passage 3	**Teacher-Directed** • Exercise 4a • Exercise 4b: Focus Lesson • Vocabulary Power! 3 • Thor, Emily, and the Little Successor, Ch. 3 • Guide practice, as needed, on Comp & Skill 5, 6a, and 6b **Independent Work** • On Your Own: Partner or Whisper Read, Thor, Emily, and the Little Successor, Ch. 4 • Comp & Skill 5, 6a, and 6b **Homework** • Homework Passage 4
Day 5	Day 6	Day 7	Day 8
Teacher-Directed • Exercise 5 • Vocabulary Power! 4 • Tropical Rain Forest, Ch. 1 • Guide practice on Comp & Skill 7 and Science Digest Entry 3 **Independent Work** • Repeated Reading: Partner or Whisper Read, Tropical Rain Forest, Ch. 1 • Comp & Skill 7 and Digest Entry 3 **Homework** • Homework Passage 5	**Teacher-Directed** • Exercise 6 • Tropical Rain Forest, Ch. 2, pages 62–65 • Guide practice, as needed, on Comp & Skill 8 and Science Digest Entry 4 **Independent Work** • On Your Own: Partner or Whisper Read, Tropical Rain Forest, Ch. 2, pages 66–69 • Comp & Skill 8 and Science Digest Entry 4 **Homework** • Homework Passage 6	**Teacher-Directed** • Exercise 7 • Vocabulary Power! 5 • Miss Tam's Corner • Guide practice, as needed, on Comp & Skill 9 and Science Digest Entries 5a, 5b **Independent Work** • Repeated Reading: Partner or Whisper Read, Miss Tam's Corner • Comp & Skill 9 and Science Digest Entries 5a, 5b **Homework** • Homework Passage 7	**Teacher-Directed** • Exercise 8 • Fluency, Grade 3 **Independent Work** • Repeated Reading: Partner or Whisper Read, Grade 3 • Written Assessment • Oral Reading Fluency Assessment* **Homework** • Homework Passage 8

Note: Unit 23 features an extra Just for Fun Comp & Skill activity, located after Activity 1. This page can be used any time during the unit.

* The Oral Reading Fluency Assessments are individually administered by the teacher while students are working on their Written Assessments.

10-DAY PLAN

Day 1	Day 2	Day 3	Day 4	Day 5
Teacher-Directed • Exercise 1 • Unit Opener • Letter From the Editor • Vocabulary Power! 1 • Antarctica! • Guide practice, as needed, on Comp & Skill 1 and Science Digest Entries 1a, 1b, 1c **Independent Work** • Repeated Reading: Partner or Whisper Read, Antarctica! • Comp & Skill 1 and Science Digest Entries 1a, 1b, 1c **Homework** • Homework Passage 1	**Teacher-Directed** • Exercise 2a • Exercise 2b: Focus Lesson • What's Black and White and Royalty? • A Penguin's Calendar • Guide practice, as needed, on Comp & Skill 2 and Science Digest Entries 2a, 2b **Independent Work** • Repeated Reading: Partner or Whisper Read, What's Black and White and Royalty? • Comp & Skill 2 and Science Digest Entries 2a, 2b **Homework** • Homework Passage 2	**Teacher-Directed** • Exercise 3 • Vocabulary Power! 2 • Thor, Emily, and the Little Successor, Ch. 1 • Guide practice, as needed, on Comp & Skill 3, 4 **Independent Work** • On Your Own: Partner or Whisper Read, Thor, Emily, and the Little Successor, Ch. 2 • Comp & Skill 3 and 4 **Homework** • Homework Passage 3	**Teacher-Directed** • Exercise 4a • Exercise 4b: Focus Lesson • Vocabulary Power! 3 • Thor, Emily, and the Little Successor, Ch. 3 • Guide practice, as needed, on Comp & Skill 5 **Independent Work** • Repeated Reading: Partner or Whisper Read, Thor, Emily, and the Little Successor, Ch. 3 • Comp & Skill 5 **Homework** • Homework Passage 4	**Teacher-Directed** • Review Exercises 4a and 4b • Review Vocabulary Power! 3 • Thor, Emily, and the Little Successor, Ch. 4 • Guide practice, as needed, on Comp & Skill 6a, 6b **Independent Work** • Repeated Reading: Partner or Whisper Read, Thor, Emily, and the Little Successor, Ch. 4 • Comp & Skill 6a and 6b **Homework** • Comp & Skill 4 (Fluency Passage)
Day 6	**Day 7**	**Day 8**	**Day 9**	**Day 10**
Teacher-Directed • Exercise 5 • Vocabulary Power! 4 • Tropical Rain Forest, Ch. 1 • Guide practice, as needed, on Comp & Skill 7 and Science Digest Entry 3 **Independent Work** • Repeated Reading: Partner or Whisper Read, Tropical Rain Forest, Ch. 1 • Comp & Skill 7 and Science Digest Entry 3 **Homework** • Homework Passage 5	**Teacher-Directed** • Exercise 6 • Review Vocabulary Power! 4 • Tropical Rain Forest, Ch. 2, pages 62–65 • Guide practice, as needed, on Comp & Skill 8 **Independent Work** • Repeated Reading: Partner or Whisper Read, Tropical Rain Forest, Ch. 2, pages 62–65 • Comp & Skill 8 **Homework** • Homework Passage 6	**Teacher-Directed** • Review Exercise 6 • Review Vocabulary Power! 4 • Tropical Rain Forest, Ch. 2, pages 66–69 • Guide practice, as needed, on Science Digest Entry 4 **Independent Work** • Repeated Reading: Partner or Whisper Read, Tropical Rain Forest, Ch. 2, pages 66–69 • Science Digest Entry 4 **Homework** • Reread Homework Passage 6	**Teacher-Directed** • Exercise 7 • Vocabulary Power! 5 • Miss Tam's Corner • Guide practice, as needed, on Comp & Skill 9 and Science Digest Entries 5a, 5b **Independent Work** • Repeated Reading: Partner or Whisper Read, Miss Tam's Corner • Comp & Skill 9 and Science Digest Entries 5a and 5b **Homework** • Homework Passage 7	**Teacher-Directed** • Exercise 8 • Fluency, Grade 3 **Independent Work** • Repeated Reading: Partner or Whisper Read, Grade 3 • Written Assessment • Oral Reading Fluency Assessment* **Homework** • Homework Passage 8

Materials and Materials Preparation

Core Lessons

Teacher Materials

READ WELL 2 MATERIALS

- Unit 23 Teacher's Guide
- Sound Cards
- Unit 23 Oral Reading Fluency Assessment found on page 144
- Group Assessment Record found in the *Assessment Manual*

SCHOOL SUPPLIES

Stopwatch or watch with a second hand

Student Materials

READ WELL 2 MATERIALS (for each student)

- *Read Well Science Digest: Where in the World*
- *Exercise Book 4*
- *Activity Book 4* or copies of Unit 23 Comprehension and Skill Work
- Unit 23 Written Assessment found in *Activity Book 4*, page 101, and on the blackline master CD
- Unit 23 Certificate of Achievement (blackline master, page 145)
- Unit 23 Homework (blackline masters)
  See *Getting Started* for suggested homework routines.

SCHOOL SUPPLIES

Pencils, colors (optional—markers, crayons, or colored pencils)

Make one copy per student of each blackline master, as appropriate for the group.

Note: For new or difficult Comprehension and Skill Activities, make overhead transparencies from the blackline masters. Use the transparencies to demonstrate and guide practice.

SPECIAL NOTE

Your students will complete a little *Science Digest* of their own. For ease of use, pull pages 29–34 from *Activity Book 4* or make double-sided copies. Fold and staple into a book.

FOCUS LESSONS

For Exercises 2b and 4b (Focus Lessons), make overhead transparencies from the blackline masters, write on transparencies placed over the pages, or use paper copies to demonstrate how to complete the lessons.

Important Tips

Pacing

Theme	Unit No.	Unit	Days in Core Plan
Earth We Share	23	RW Science Digest: Where in the World?	8
	24	Judy Moody Saves the World!	12
Mystery	25	The Absent Author	9

> **YOU ARE HERE.**
> 29+ days of instruction to the end of the program

AN EARLY FINISH

If your students began *Read Well 2* midway into the program, you may finish *Read Well 2 Plus* before the end of the school year. After completing Unit 25, *The Absent Author*, you may wish to:

1. Have students work in a 3^{-2} (mid third grade) or 4^{-1} (beginning fourth grade) basal.

2. Have students read a favorite trade book at a high third grade to fourth grade reading level.

Before guided Story Reading, preteach selected vocabulary words.
- Select new vocabulary words central to each chapter.
- Preteach vocabulary words using student-friendly definitions and examples.
- Have students use the words many times in different contexts.

> *Continue* using explicit and systematic instruction.

Before guided Story Reading, review phonics and structural word-reading skills and preteach new words.
- Use the Jell-Well Planner from the *Assessment Manual* (page 108) to develop decoding lessons. (The planner can be used for review and also to move students forward.)
- Provide ongoing review of vowel patterns and affixes using mixed lists of words from the novel.
- Select and preteach new and difficult multisyllabic words.

During guided Story Reading, have students:
- read aloud with you for 15–20 minutes each day, followed by independent reading.
- make predictions and identify important story elements or facts central to understanding the chapter. Have students make inferences and draw conclusions.
- set the purpose for independent reading by asking questions and discussing responses.

> Encourage students to use the skills and strategies they have learned throughout *Read Well 2*.

After Story Reading, have students:
- do partner reading.
- make a vocabulary log (define the word, write a sentence, draw a picture).
- use graphic organizers.
- write about their reading (response log, retells, notes and a report, fact summaries, opinions . . .).

How to Teach the Lessons

Teach from this section. Each instructional component is outlined in an easy-to-teach format.

Exercise 1

- Unit Opener: Read Well Science Digest
- Vocabulary Power! 1
- Story Reading 1
  With the Teacher: Antarctica!
- Comprehension and Skill Activity 1, Science Digest Entries 1a, 1b, 1c

Exercise 2a

- Exercise 2b, Focus Lesson
- Story Reading 2
  With the Teacher: What's Black and White and Royalty?
- Comprehension and Skill Activity 2, Science Digest Entries 2a, 2b

Exercise 3

- Vocabulary Power! 2
- Story Reading 3
  With the Teacher: Thor, Emily, and the Little Successor, Chapter 1
  On Your Own: Thor, Emily, and the Little Successor, Chapter 2
- Comprehension and Skill Activities 3 and 4

Exercise 4a

- Exercise 4b, Focus Lesson
- Vocabulary Power! 3
- Story Reading 4
  With the Teacher: Thor, Emily, and the Little Successor, Chapter 3
  On Your Own: Thor, Emily, and the Little Successor, Chapter 4
- Comprehension and Skill Activities 5, 6a, 6b

Note: Lessons include daily homework.

Exercise 5

- Vocabulary Power! 4
- Story Reading 5
  With the Teacher: Tropical Rain Forest, Chapter 1
- Comprehension and Skill Activity 7, Science Digest Entry 3

Exercise 6

- Story Reading 6
  With the Teacher: Tropical Rain Forest, Chapter 2, pages 62–65
  On Your Own: Tropical Rain Forest, Chapter 2, pages 66–69
- Comprehension and Skill Activity 8, Science Digest Entry 4

Exercise 7

- Vocabulary Power! 5
- Story Reading 7
  With the Teacher: Miss Tam's Corner
- Comprehension and Skill Activity 9, Science Digest Entries 5a, 5b

Exercise 8

- Story Reading 8 (Excerise Book)
  With the Teacher: Grade 3 (Fluency)
- Written Assessment

❶ SOUND REVIEW

PACING

Exercise 1 should take about 15 minutes.

❷ SOUND PRACTICE

- For each task, have students spell and say the focus sound in the gray bar.
- Next, have students read each underlined sound, the word, then the whole column.
- Repeat with each column, building accuracy first, then fluency.

❸ SHIFTY WORDS

BUILD ACCURACY AND FLUENCY (Reminder)

For all rows and columns, follow the specific directions, then build accuracy and fluency with whole words.

❹ ACCURACY AND FLUENCY BUILDING

B1. Related Words

- Tell students the first set of words is related to the word "cold." Have them read the words.
- Repeat with "edit." Use the words in sentences, as needed.

edit	I will check and correct my paper. I will . . . *edit* . . . it.
editing	I was very careful when I was . . . *editing* . . . my paper.
editor	A person who edits is an . . . *editor*.
edition	We don't get the afternoon edition of the newspaper. We get the morning . . . *edition*.

C1. Multisyllabic Words

- For the list of words divided by syllables, have students read each syllable, then the whole word. Use the word in a sentence, as appropriate.
- For the list of whole words, build accuracy and then fluency.

equator	An imaginary circle around the Earth, midway between the North and South Poles, is the . . . *equator*.
Arctic	Polar bears live in the most northern part of the world, called the . . . *Arctic*.
Antarctica	The Earth's most southern continent is . . . *Antarctica*.

E1. Tricky Words

- For each Tricky Word, have students use the sounds and word parts they know to silently sound out the word. Use the word in a sentence to help with pronunciation.
- If the word is unfamiliar, tell students the word.

lichens
Look at the first word. The word is *lichens*. Say the word. (lichens) The plants growing on the rocks are . . . *lichens*. Read the word two times. (lichens, lichens)

unique	Everyone's fingerprints are different. They are . . . *unique*.
algae	The green, slimy plants on the side of the fish tank are . . . *algae*.
movies	Let's get some popcorn when we go to the . . . *movies*.
hero	The brave police officer was my . . . *hero*.

zero
Look at the next word. The word rhymes with *hero*. Read the word. (zero)
The kids sold all their candy bars. They had . . . *zero* . . . candy bars left.
Read the word three times. (zero, zero, zero)

- Have students go back and read the whole words in the column.

❺ WORD ENDINGS

6 MORPHOGRAPHS AND AFFIXES

7 GENERALIZATION: READING NEW WORDS IN PARAGRAPHS
- Have students read the paragraph silently, then out loud. Tell students to use the sounds and word parts they know to read any difficult words.
- Repeat practice, as needed.

Science Digest: Where in the World?

Unit 23 Exercise 1
Use before Antarctica

1. SOUND REVIEW Use selected Sound Cards from Units 1–19.

2. SOUND PRACTICE In each column, have students spell and say the sound, next say any underlined sound and the word, then read the column.

oa	-ture	ee, ea	-le	e as in Ed
c**oa**st	litera**ture**	Gr**ee**ks	litt**le**	m**e**lts
r**oa**med	crea**ture**	degr**ee**s	midd**le**	cl**e**ver
b**oa**st	fea**ture**	t**ea**ses	jung**le**	coll**e**cted

3. SHIFTY WORDS Have students read the words.

blowing	snowing	snoring	storing	boring

4. ACCURACY/FLUENCY BUILDING For each column, have students say any underlined part, then read each word. Next, have them read the column.

A1 Mixed Practice	B1 Related Words	C1 Multisyllabic Words	D1 Multisyllabic Words	E1 Tricky Words
dr**i**fted	cold	e·qua·tor	blizzard	lichens
vall**eys**	colder	Arc·tic	librarian	unique
v**o**lume	coldest	Ant·arc·ti·ca	planet	algae
s**ai**ling			wildlife	movies
bl**a**sts	edit	equator	secret	
thr**i**lled	editing	Arctic	fossils	hero
	editor	Antarctica		zero
	edition			

5. WORD ENDINGS Have students read the word, then the word with an ending.

ice icy	windy windiest	dry driest

6. MORPHOGRAPHS AND AFFIXES Have students read each underlined part, then the word.

rare**ly**	danger**ous**	exped**it**ion	bottom**less**	enjoy**able**

7. GENERALIZATION Have students read the paragraph silently, then out loud. (New words: explorer, Antarctic, freezing, landscape)

The explorer went to the Antarctic region to study the frozen landscape. The freezing temperatures were harsh. The icy winds were the coldest he had ever felt. He could not wait to get home to feel warm again.

TEAM EXPECTATIONS (Reminder)

Provide a quick review of expectations before starting the lesson.
1. Sit up.
2. Follow directions.
3. Help each other.
4. Work hard and have fun.

ACKNOWLEDGE STUDENTS WHEN THEY MEET YOUR EXPECTATIONS

Students respond positively when you acknowledge their accomplishments. Pair descriptive praise with an individual turn or job. [Candace], great job sitting up and finger tracking. You have a professional attitude about your learning. Everyone, watch how [Candace] is able to follow along while I read.

GENERALIZATION (Reminder)

The generalization task provides an opportunity for you to informally assess students' ability to read new words that have not been pretaught.

COMPREHENSION PROCESSES

Remember, Understand, Apply

PROCEDURES

1. **Introducing the Magazine**

   Identifying—Title, What; Inferring
   Have students identify the title of their magazine. Say something like:
   Today, we get to read a new edition of the Read Well Science Digest.
   What's the title of your magazine?
   (Science Digest)

   Let's look at the cover lines on the front of your Science Digest. *Look at the circle. It tells you what the whole magazine is about. What does it say?* (Where in the world?)

   That's the theme, or big idea, of this Science Digest. Now read the next question. I'll start the question with "Where in the world."
   Where in the world is . . . (an animal that walks 125 miles to lay an egg?)
   That's hard to imagine.

   We'll get to find out.
   Let's read the next question.
   Where in the world is . . . (a clever cat that teases fish?)
   That's an interesting question.

   This should be a very interesting magazine.
   What else are we going to find out about?
   (Where in the world is a desert made of ice?)

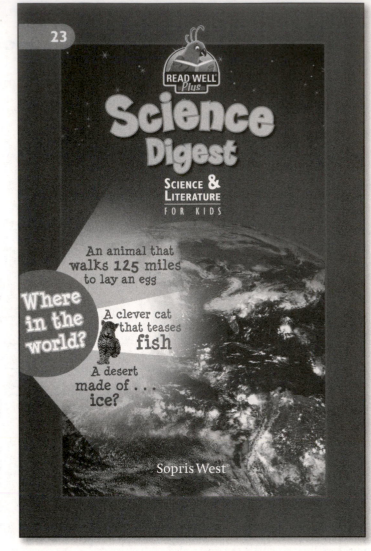

2. Using the Table of Contents

Using the Table of Contents; Inferring—Topic; Identifying—Titles, What; Viewing

Have students look at the Table of Contents. Say something like:

Turn to the Table of Contents.

In magazines, the Table of Contents looks a little different, but it still helps us find out what we're going to read about and where it's located.

The first things listed in the Table of Contents are the departments. The page number is listed first. Find the "Letter From the Editor."

What page is it on? (page 5)

Where will you find "Vocabulary Power! 2"? (page 28)

Find the words *Features, Nonfiction*.

How many articles are there? (three)

What are we going to read about? (Antarctica, penguins)

TABLE OF CONTENTS

UNIT 23 • Where in the World?

Turn to page 4 of the Table of Contents. What are you going to read on page 54? (Tropical Rain Forest)

Yes, you're going to read about the rain forest.

This magazine also has a special feature called "Miss Tam's Corner." What page is it on? (page 72)

Look at the photos in the circles. What do you see in the top circle? (a bird)

What do you see in the next circle?

(a snake)

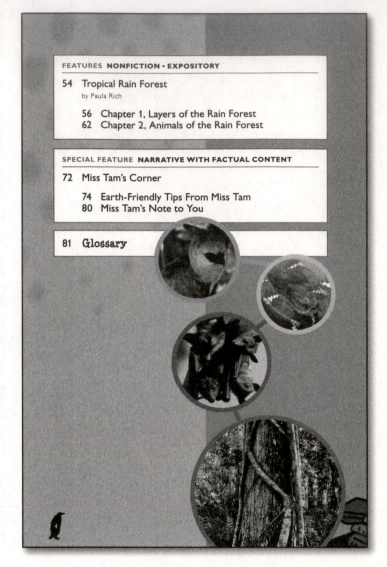

3. Introducing the Letter From the Editor

Identifying—Who

- Explain what an editor and a letter from the editor are. Say something like:
  Look at page 5. The first thing we're going to read today is the "Letter From the Editor."
  Who is the letter from? (The letter is from the editor.)

  The editor of a magazine is in charge of everything that goes in the magazine. In the "Letter From the Editor," the editor talks to the readers. Who is the editor talking to? (The editor is talking to us, the readers.)

  Look at the picture and the signature at the bottom of the letter. Who is the guest editor of this edition of the magazine?
  (Miss Tam)

  I love Miss Tam. This should be a great magazine.

- Have students read the letter from the editor. Mix group and individual turns.

WITH THE TEACHER

Letter From the Editor

Dear Readers:

You can imagine how thrilled Minnie Bird, Scraggly Cat, and I were when I was named guest editor for this edition of the *Read Well Science Digest*.

We think the Earth we share is an amazing planet. We didn't know what in the world we wanted to write about. Ghana? Hawaii? Montgomery? We decided to feature the coldest, driest, windiest place on Earth and the wettest places on Earth. We hope you enjoy "Where in the World?"

Yours truly,
Miss Tam, Guest Editor
Retired Librarian and World Traveler

5

COMPREHENSION PROCESSES
Understand, Apply

PROCEDURES

1. Introducing Vocabulary

> ★ freezing ★ blizzard
> ★ equator ★ Arctic
> ★ Antarctic ★ harsh
> ★ temperature, unique

- For each vocabulary word, have students read the word by parts, then read the whole word.
- Read the student-friendly explanations to students as they follow with their fingers. Then have students use the vocabulary word by following the gray text.
- Review and discuss the photos and illustrations.

USING VOCABULARY

WITH THE TEACHER

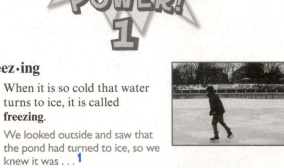

VOCABULARY POWER! 1

★ **freez·ing**

When it is so cold that water turns to ice, it is called **freezing**.

We looked outside and saw that the pond had turned to ice, so we knew it was . . . **1**

★ **bliz·zard**

When it is snowing and the wind is blowing hard, it is called a **blizzard**.

The news report said schools were closed because of the *blizzard*. Describe what the weather was like. **2**

★ **e·qua·tor**

If you drew a line around the middle of the Earth, that would be the **equator**.

If you stand at the *equator*, it is the same distance to the top of the Earth and the bottom of the Earth. Look at the globe and trace your finger along the equator. What do you know about the equator? **3**

★ = New

6

❶ **Understand:** Using Vocabulary—freezing (freezing)

❷ **Understand:** Defining and Using Vocabulary—blizzard (There was a blizzard. It was snowing, and the wind was blowing hard.)

❸ **Understand:** Demonstrating; Defining and Using Vocabulary—equator (The equator is an imaginary line around the middle of the Earth.)

★ = New in this unit

2. Now You Try It!

- Read or paraphrase the directions.
- Have students read each word by parts, then read the whole word.
- Have students explain or define the words in their own words. Say something like:

  Look at the first word. Say the parts, then read the whole word.

  (tem•per•a•ture, temperature)

  Now let's pretend that we're going to explain or define the word *temperature* to a friend. [Maria], what would you say?

  Start with "The *temperature* . . ." (The temperature tells you how hot or cold it is.)

  That's right. The temperature tells us how hot or cold it is.

- Have students turn to the appropriate page in the glossary and discuss how their definition is the same as or different from the glossary's. Your students may like their definition better.

Note: By defining a word in their own words, students are demonstrating depth of word knowledge. Verbatim responses only demonstrate memorization. Encourage paraphrasing.

ANTARCTICA!

★ **Arc·tic**

The **Arctic** is the area at the top of the Earth.

The *Arctic* is a very cold area. If you went on an expedition there, what would you need to bring?[1]

★ **Ant·arc·tic**

The **Antarctic** is the land at the bottom of the Earth.

The *Antarctic* is another name for the continent of Antarctica. Touch Antarctica.[2]

★ **harsh**

Something is **harsh** when it is uncomfortable, difficult, or rough!

Antarctica has the *harshest* weather in the world. Do you know what that means?[3]

Now You Try It!

Try defining the next words. Then look up the words in the glossary. Your definition might be better!

★ **tem·per·a·ture**

Start with "The *temperature* tells us . . ."[4]
Let's find the word on page 86.

u·nique

Start with "Something that is *unique* is . . ."[5]
Let's find the word on page 87.

USING VOCABULARY

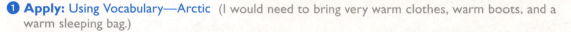

1 Apply: Using Vocabulary—Arctic (I would need to bring very warm clothes, warm boots, and a warm sleeping bag.)

2 Apply: Demonstrating; Using Vocabulary—Antarctic

3 Apply: Using Vocabulary—harshest (It means that Antarctica must be the coldest place in the world. It must have weather that is worse than any other place . . .)

4 Understand: Defining and Using Vocabulary—temperature; Using Glossary (The temperature tells us how hot or cold it is.)

5 Understand: Defining and Using Vocabulary—unique; Using Glossary (Something that is unique is very special. It is one of a kind.)

STORY READING 1 INSTRUCTIONS

Students read "Antarctica!" on pages 8–17 with the teacher.

COMPREHENSION PROCESSES

Remember, Understand, Apply, Analyze, Create

COMPREHENSION BUILDING

- Encourage students to answer questions with complete sentences.
- If students have difficulty comprehending, think aloud with them or reread the portion of the story that answers the question. Repeat the question.

PROCEDURES

1. Introducing the Article

> **Viewing; Identifying—Who, What, Title**
> Say something like:
> Turn to pages 8 and 9. Look at the picture. What do you see?
> (Earth—the blue planet, astronauts, Miss Tam, Scraggly Cat, and Minnie Bird)
> This page gives us a riddle. "Where in the World is . . .
> Touch the first bullet and read. (the coldest continent?)
> Repeat with each bullet.
> Find the answer. What does it say? (Answer: It's the continent at the bottom of the world.)
> Find the title. It's . . . Antarctica!

> **CORRECTING DECODING ERRORS**
>
> During story reading, gently correct any error, then have students reread the sentence.

2. First Reading

- Ask questions and discuss the text as indicated by the gray text.
- Mix group and individual turns, independent of your voice.
  Have students work toward a group accuracy goal of 0–6 errors.
  Quietly keep track of errors made by all students in the group.
- After reading the story, practice any difficult words.
  Repeat, if students have not reached the accuracy goal.

3. Second Reading, Short Passage Practice: Developing Prosody

- Demonstrate expressive, fluent reading of the first two paragraphs.
- Guide practice with your voice.
- Provide individual turns while others track with their fingers and whisper read.
- Repeat with one paragraph at a time.

4. Partner or Whisper Reading: Repeated Reading

Before beginning independent work, have students finger track and partner or whisper read.

5. Comprehension and Skill Work

Tell students they will do Comprehension and Skill Activity 1 and start work on their own Science Digest after they read "Antarctica!" Guide practice, as needed. For teacher directions, see pages 32–35.

6. Homework 1: Repeated Reading

WITH THE TEACHER

Where in the World is...

- the coldest continent?
- the windiest continent?
- the driest continent?
- the coldest, windiest, and driest continent?

8

Antarctica!
by Susan Blackaby

Answer: It's the continent at the bottom of the world.

9

A SPECIAL NOTE FROM THE AUTHORS TO THE KIDS

Dear Readers:

The *Read Well Science Digest* is the work of many people working together. Many authors and who else? That's right—editors, illustrators . . . There are many other very important people as well. People who put the articles, photos, and illustrations together are called designers. Our lead storybook and Science Digest designer is Anne Bridgins. It was Ms. Bridgins' idea to put Miss Tam, Scraggly Cat, and Minnie Bird in the picture. Wasn't that cool?

Ms. Bridgins likes Miss Tam. She even dressed up as Miss Tam for Halloween. Give Ms. Bridgins a big hand! She won't be able to hear you, but she will be happy that you like her work. Enjoy!

Sincerely,

Marilyn Sprick, Ann Watanabe, Karen Akiyama-Paik, and Shelley V. Jones

WITH THE TEACHER

Coldest Place on Earth

The coldest place on Earth is the continent of Antarctica. A thick sheet of ice more than 7,000 feet deep covers most of the land. On a winter's day, the temperature can drop to 100 degrees below zero! That is colder than freezing—colder than any of us can imagine. Even in the summer, the temperature is rarely above freezing, so the ice never melts.

What makes Antarctica's temperature unique? 1

10

COMPREHENDING AS YOU GO

❶ **Apply:** Inferring; Explaining; Using Vocabulary—Antarctica, temperature, unique (Antarctica's temperature is unique because it is the coldest place on Earth. It can be as cold as 100 degrees below zero.)

ANTARCTICA!

Driest Place on Earth

The driest place on Earth is Antarctica. People
think it is a wet place because of the ice, but only
about two inches of rain or snow fall each year. It's
hard to believe, but the world's largest desert is in
Antarctica. It is cold and dry.

What makes Antarctica the driest place on Earth?**1**

11

**COMPREHENDING
AS YOU GO**

1 **Apply:** Inferring; Explaining; Using Vocabulary—Antarctica (Antarctica gets only two
inches of rain or snow each year. It has the world's largest desert.)

WITH THE TEACHER

Windiest Place on Earth

The windiest place on Earth is also Antarctica.
Blizzards sweep across the ice. When the winds blow,
the icy blasts make it feel even colder.

Describe Antarctica.
Why would it be difficult to survive in Antarctica?[1]

12

**COMPREHENDING
AS YOU GO**

1 **Understand:** Describing; **Apply:** Inferring, Explaining; Using Vocabulary—Antarctica, survive, harsh
(It would be hard to survive there because it is so cold. You would be freezing all the time. If you were an
animal, you would not be able to find water to drink. The wind would blow you over! It would be a harsh
place to try to live . . .)

ANTARCTICA!

Who Am I?

I am a unique animal. I am the only creature that can live in the coldest, driest, and windiest place on Earth during the harsh winter months. Who am I?**1**

COMPREHENDING AS YOU GO

❶ Apply: Making Connections; **Create:** Generating Ideas
From the riddle, we know that there is an animal that can survive in the Antarctic winter. The question is, "Who am I?" What animal do you think is asking the question?
(A penguin, a polar bear, a person . . .)

When Antarctica Was Warmer

Antarctica wasn't always so cold, so dry, and so windy. The land has changed over time.

About 500 million years ago, the land that is now Antarctica was closer to the equator. Plants covered its hills and valleys. Dinosaurs roamed from coast to coast.

ANTARCTICA
500 MILLION
YEARS AGO

This is how Earth looked long ago.

How do you think scientists know there were once dinosaurs on Antarctica?[1]

14

COMPREHENDING
AS YOU GO

① **Analyze:** Drawing Conclusions; **Apply:** Using Vocabulary—Antarctica, fossil (They must have found dinosaur fossils on Antarctica.)

ANTARCTICA!

Slowly, over millions of years, the land drifted south and became colder and colder. Now Antarctica is at the bottom of the world, and it is the coldest place on Earth.

ANTARCTICA
TODAY

Who Am I?

Little by little, Antarctica became the frozen place I call home. It went from a jungle to a vast, empty, ice-covered landscape. Now the only other living things that grow in my Antarctic home are tiny animals like worms and small lichens, moss, and algae.

15

FOCUS ON DRAWING CONCLUSIONS
Identifying—What; Inferring

After reading the page, ask students what they learned from the riddle.

Say something like:
We still don't know who the mystery animal is. What other life can survive in Antarctica? (lichen, moss, and algae) Hmmm . . . none of those are animals. The mystery animal is an animal, so what do you know about it? (It's the only animal that can survive in Antarctica.)

WITH THE TEACHER

Finding Antarctica

About 2,000 years ago, the Greeks thought there must be land at both ends of the Earth—the Arctic and Antarctic. But for thousands of years, no person set foot on Antarctica. About 500 years ago, when explorers finally proved Earth was round, people began looking for Antarctica. Sailing into the icy waters was very dangerous. No one was sure that Antarctica was really there until 1820.

Why did explorers look for Antarctica? **1**

COMPREHENDING AS YOU GO

Crossing the Ice

Once people knew where Antarctica was, they wanted to find out more about it. The first explorers came by sea. They left their boats and traveled across the freezing land in sleds. They climbed mountains. They made maps. They collected rocks. (There were fossils in some of the rocks.) The explorers also discovered new wildlife.

Do you think exploring Antarctica was easy or hard? Why? **2**

16

❶ Apply: Inferring, Explaining; Using Vocabulary—Antarctica (The Greeks thought there was land at the top of the Earth and at the bottom. Once explorers proved the Earth was round, they began to look for Antarctica.)

❷ Analyze: Drawing Conclusions; **Apply:** Using Vocabulary—Antarctica, survive (It was very hard. It's very cold there, and there were no roads or trails or wood to burn to keep warm. They had to cross the ice and carry everything they needed to survive.)

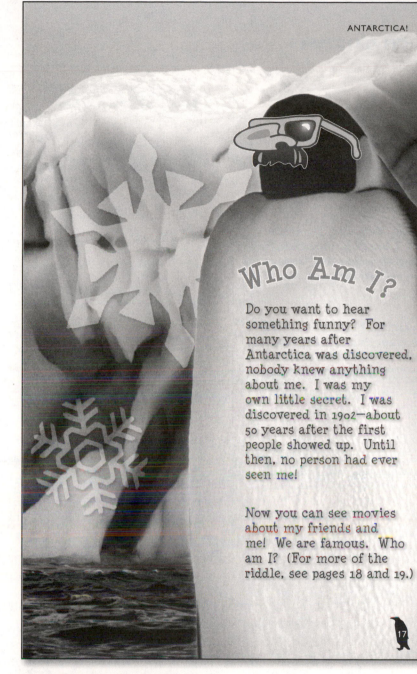

ANTARCTICA!

Who Am I?

Do you want to hear something funny? For many years after Antarctica was discovered, nobody knew anything about me. I was my own little secret. I was discovered in 1902—about 50 years after the first people showed up. Until then, no person had ever seen me!

Now you can see movies about my friends and me! We are famous. Who am I? (For more of the riddle, see pages 18 and 19.)

17

After Reading Page 17

1 Remember: Identifying—What
What else did you learn from the riddle about the mystery animal?
(Even after people found Antarctica, no one knew about it.)

2 Create: Generating Ideas
That's right. No one knew it existed. Why do you think that might be?
(It was too small to see. It was well camouflaged.)

3 Analyze: Drawing Conclusions
The mystery animal is also seen in movies now. Think of an animal that we see in movies that lives in a cold and frozen place. What might it be?
(a penguin, a polar bear . . .)

4 Remember: Locating Information; **Apply:** Inferring
Where should we go to find more of the riddle? (pages 18 and 19)
Look at pages 18 and 19. Which animal do you think our mystery animal is?
(the penguin, the whale, the goose . . .)

FACT SUMMARY

COMPREHENSION PROCESSES

Remember, Understand

WRITING TRAITS

Organization—Topic Sentence, Supporting Details
Conventions—Complete Sentence, Capital, Period
Presentation

Using Graphic Organizer
Locating Information
Identifying—Supporting Details
Using Vocabulary—Antarctica, harsh

Summarizing—Main Idea/Topic
Supporting Details/Facts
Using Vocabulary—Antarctica, harsh
Sentence Writing

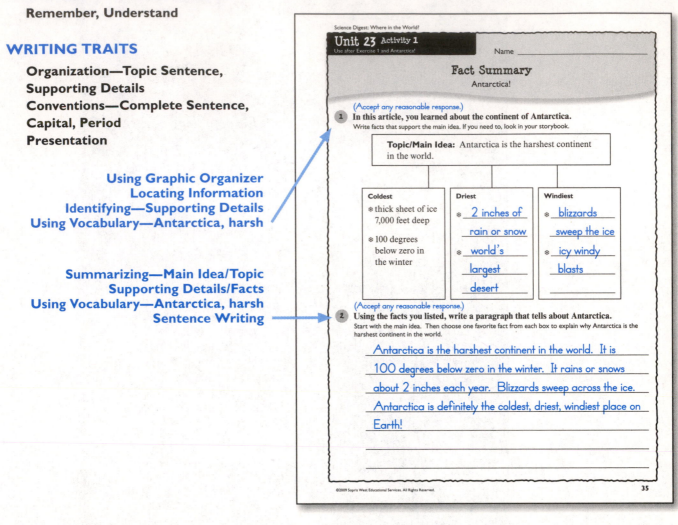

Science Digest: Where in the World?

Unit 23 Activity 1
Use after Exercise 1 and Antarctica!

Name _____

Fact Summary
Antarctica!

(Accept any reasonable response.)

1 **In this article, you learned about the continent of Antarctica.**
Write facts that support the main idea. If you need to, look in your storybook.

Topic/Main Idea: Antarctica is the harshest continent in the world.

Coldest
* thick sheet of ice 7,000 feet deep
* 100 degrees below zero in the winter

Driest
* 2 inches of rain or snow
* world's largest desert

Windiest
* blizzards sweep the ice
* icy windy blasts

(Accept any reasonable response.)

2 **Using the facts you listed, write a paragraph that tells about Antarctica.**
Start with the main idea. Then choose one favorite fact from each box to explain why Antarctica is the harshest continent in the world.

Antarctica is the harshest continent in the world. It is 100 degrees below zero in the winter. It rains or snows about 2 inches each year. Blizzards sweep across the ice. Antarctica is definitely the coldest, driest, windiest place on Earth!

35

PROCEDURES

For each step, demonstrate and guide practice, as needed. Then have students complete the page independently.

1. **Main Idea/Supporting Details: Hierarchy Chart—Basic Instructions** (Item 1)
   - Have students read the topic/main idea.
   - Have students complete the facts about Antarctica.

2. **Fact Summary: Paragraph Writing—Basic Instructions** (Item 2)
   Have students write a fact summary paragraph with the facts from Item 1. Assist, only as needed.

Self-monitoring
Have students check and correct their work.

JUST FOR FUN • WORLD MAP

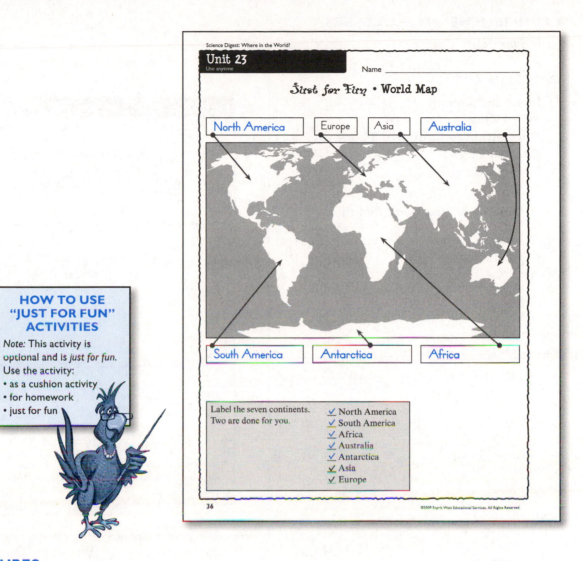

HOW TO USE "JUST FOR FUN" ACTIVITIES

Note: This activity is optional and is *just for fun.* Use the activity:
• as a cushion activity
• for homework
• just for fun

PROCEDURES

As time allows, have students label the seven continents on the world map, using the content names provided in the box. This page may be given to students as homework.

ENTRY 1a

COMPREHENSION PROCESSES

Understand, Create

WRITING TRAITS

**Ideas and Content
Word Choice
Conventions—Complete Sentence,
Capital, Period
Presentation**

**Following Directions; Identifying—
Author**

PROCEDURES

Have students complete the page independently. Guide practice, only as needed.

Cover—Specific Instructions (Entry 1a)

Have students write their name on the cover as the author.

Note: Tell students they will illustrate the cover after they've completed their Science Digest. Explain that the cover of a magazine or storybook is usually completed after the designers know what the whole magazine or storybook is about.

SPECIAL NOTE

Your students will complete a little *Science Digest* of their own. For ease of use, pull pages 29–34 from *Activity Book 4*. Fold and staple into a book.

ENTRIES 1b, 1c

Locating Information; Using Table of Contents

Generating Ideas, Sentence Writing, Sentence Completion

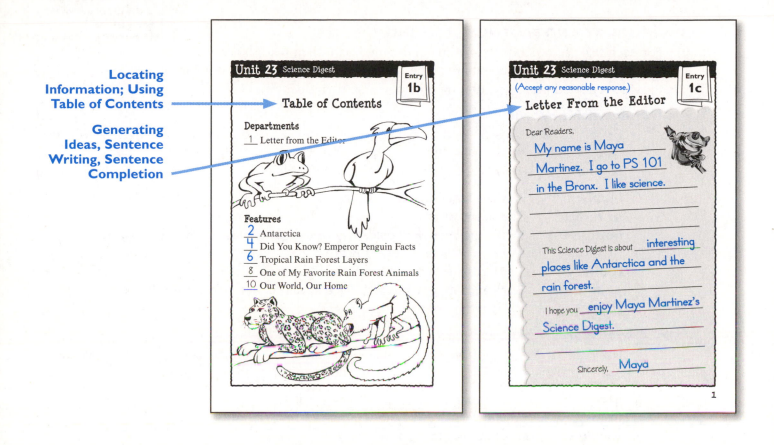

Table of Contents—Specific Instructions (Entry 1b)

Have students find the page numbers for each department and feature and write the correct page number in the blank.

Letter Writing: Creative Writing—Specific Instructions (Entry 1c)

Have students write a letter to their readers. Encourage them to use snazzy vocabulary words. Remind them to start sentences with a capital and end with a period.

❶ SOUND REVIEW

Have students read the sounds and key word phrases. Work for accuracy, then fluency.

PACING

Exercise 2a should take about 10 minutes, allowing about 10 minutes for the Focus Lesson.

❷ ACCURACY AND FLUENCY BUILDING

• For each task, have students say any underlined part, then read the word.
• Set a pace. Then have students read the whole words in each task and column.
• Provide repeated practice, building accuracy first, then fluency.

C1. Multisyllabic Words

• For the list of words divided by syllables, have students read each syllable, then the whole word. Use the word in a sentence, as appropriate.
• For the list of whole words, build accuracy and then fluency.

blubber	A whale has a thick layer of fat called . . . *blubber.*
Antarctic	The scientists are studying the . . . *Antarctic* . . . region.
huddle	When the boys were cold, they would gather close to the campfire. They would . . . *huddle* . . . near the fire.
rookery	The birds' nesting area is called a . . . *rookery.*
penguins	Black and white Antarctic birds that can survive in freezing cold are . . . *penguins.*
royalty	Kings and queens are . . . *royalty.*

D1. Tricky Words

• For each Tricky Word, have students use the sounds and word parts they know to silently sound out the word. Use the word in a sentence to help with pronunciation.

group	The three boys are working together in a . . . *group.*
field	Wildflowers covered the . . . *field.*
warmest	It will be cold today, so wear your . . . *warmest* . . . coat.
though	Evan kept playing soccer, even . . . *though* . . . it started to rain.
through	The crack was too small for the mouse to wiggle . . . *through.*

• Have students go back and read the whole words in the column.

❸ WORDS IN CONTEXT

For each word, have students use the sounds and word parts they know to silently sound out the word. Then have students read the sentence. Assist, as needed.

❹ WORD ENDINGS

Have students read any underlined word, then the word with an ending.

❺ MORPHOGRAPHS AND AFFIXES

• Have students read the underlined part, then the whole word.
• Repeat practice with whole words, mixing group and individual turns. Build accuracy, then fluency.

❻ GENERALIZATION: READING NEW WORDS IN PARAGRAPHS

• Have students read the paragraph silently, then out loud. Tell students to use the sounds and word parts they know to read any difficult words.
• Repeat practice, as needed.

Science Digest: Where in the World?

Unit 23 Exercise 2a
Use before What's Black and White and Royalty? and A Penguin's Calendar

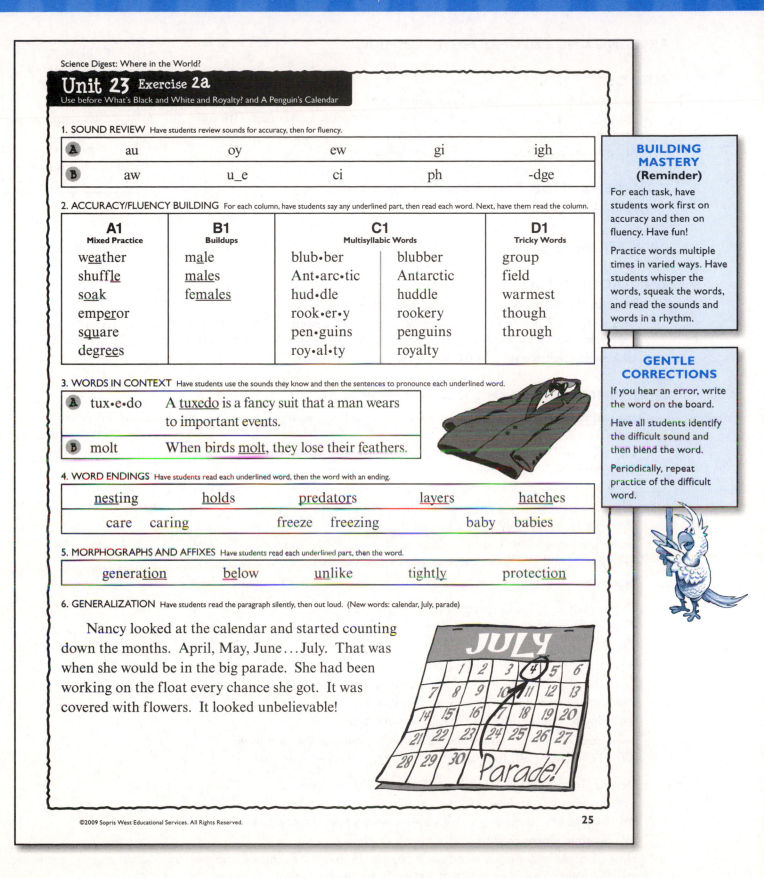

1. SOUND REVIEW Have students review sounds for accuracy, then for fluency.

A	au	oy	ew	gi	igh
B	aw	u_e	ci	ph	-dge

2. ACCURACY/FLUENCY BUILDING For each column, have students say any underlined part, then read each word. Next, have them read the column.

A1 Mixed Practice	B1 Buildups	C1 Multisyllabic Words		D1 Tricky Words
w<u>ea</u>ther	m<u>a</u>l<u>e</u>	blub•ber	blubber	group
shuff<u>le</u>	m<u>a</u>l<u>es</u>	Ant•arc•tic	Antarctic	field
s<u>oa</u>k	fem<u>a</u>l<u>es</u>	hud•dle	huddle	warmest
emp<u>e</u>ror		rook•er•y	rookery	though
sq<u>ua</u>re		pen•guins	penguins	through
degr<u>ee</u>s		roy•al•ty	royalty	

3. WORDS IN CONTEXT Have students use the sounds they know and then the sentences to pronounce each underlined word.

A	tux•e•do	A <u>tuxedo</u> is a fancy suit that a man wears to important events.
B	molt	When birds <u>molt</u>, they lose their feathers.

4. WORD ENDINGS Have students read each underlined word, then the word with an ending.

<u>n</u>esting   holds   <u>predators</u>   <u>layers</u>   <u>hatches</u>

care   caring   freeze   freezing   baby   babies

5. MORPHOGRAPHS AND AFFIXES Have students read each underlined part, then the word.

genera<u>tion</u>   <u>below</u>   <u>un</u>like   tight<u>ly</u>   protec<u>tion</u>

6. GENERALIZATION Have students read the paragraph silently, then out loud. (New words: calendar, July, parade)

Nancy looked at the calendar and started counting down the months. April, May, June…July. That was when she would be in the big parade. She had been working on the float every chance she got. It was covered with flowers. It looked unbelievable!

25

BUILDING MASTERY (Reminder)

For each task, have students work first on accuracy and then on fluency. Have fun!

Practice words multiple times in varied ways. Have students whisper the words, squeak the words, and read the sounds and words in a rhythm.

GENTLE CORRECTIONS

If you hear an error, write the word on the board.

Have all students identify the difficult sound and then blend the word.

Periodically, repeat practice of the difficult word.

REVISING AND EDITING: FACT SUMMARY

PREP NOTES

Use an overhead of the Antarctica fact summary found in the *Exercise Book* on page 26.

PURPOSE

This lesson provides explicit instruction in how to revise and edit a fact summary draft. The lesson prepares students to edit and finalize their Comprehension and Skill Activity 1 Fact Summary paragraphs, which they will copy on Entry 2a in their Science Digest.

PACING

Exercise 2b should take 10–15 minutes.

COMPREHENSION PROCESSES

Understand, Create

PROCEDURES

❶ INTRODUCTION

- Explain the purpose of the lesson. Say something like:

  This lesson will help you make your Antarctica fact summary from Comprehension and Skill Activity 1 even better. Good writers go back to what they have written and make it snazzier. They make their sentences sophisticated by using snazzy words.

❷ ADDING MORE SOPHISTICATED WORDS

Generating Ideas; Using Vocabulary—harsh, unique, temperature, fascinate, ecosystem, vast, impressive, freezing

- Use the overhead of the fact summary paragraph (see Prep Notes above) to guide how to check for clarity.

  Look at your focus lesson. It has my fact summary on it. Read number one in the check and correct box. (Does your summary make sense?) Everyone read my paragraph. Let's see if it makes sense. (Antarctica is the hashest continent in the world . . .) Did it make sense? (almost)

  [Jerod], what do I need to fix? (You need to fix *harshest.* It says, "hashest.")

  Excellent catch! Everyone, how should I spell *harshest*?

  Demonstrate how to cross out "hashest" with one line and write "harshest" above it.

- Guide checking for corrections.

  Read number two in the check and correct box. (Do you have any corrections to make?)

  Were there other corrections I need to make? (no) So I can check off the first and second box.

  Read the directions for number three. (Does your paragraph have . . .)

  Read the words in the word bank. (harshest, unique, temperature . . .)

  What snazzy words are already in my paragraph? (harshest, temperature)

  I'm going to circle those words on my word bank.

  Demonstrate how to circle "harshest" and "temperature" in the word bank.

  Now I can check off the third box.

- Demonstrate and guide adding snazzy words to your draft.

  What does the last direction say? (Add a snazzy word or two.)

  I'm going to try to make my fact summary even better by adding a snazzy word or two.

  What other words might I use? (unique, fascinate . . .)

  Hmm, I could include the word *unique* by saying that "It *is unique because it* rains or snows only about two inches a year." I'll use a caret and add in "is unique because it."

  Demonstrate how to use a caret to make the third sentence begin "It is unique because it . . . "

  Great job! I can check off the last box. I have a summary I'll be proud of.

- Tell students they will edit and carefully copy their own summaries into their Science Digest.

Science Digest: Where in the World?

Unit 23 Exercise **2b** (Focus Lesson)
Use after Exercise 2a and before What's Black and White and Royalty?

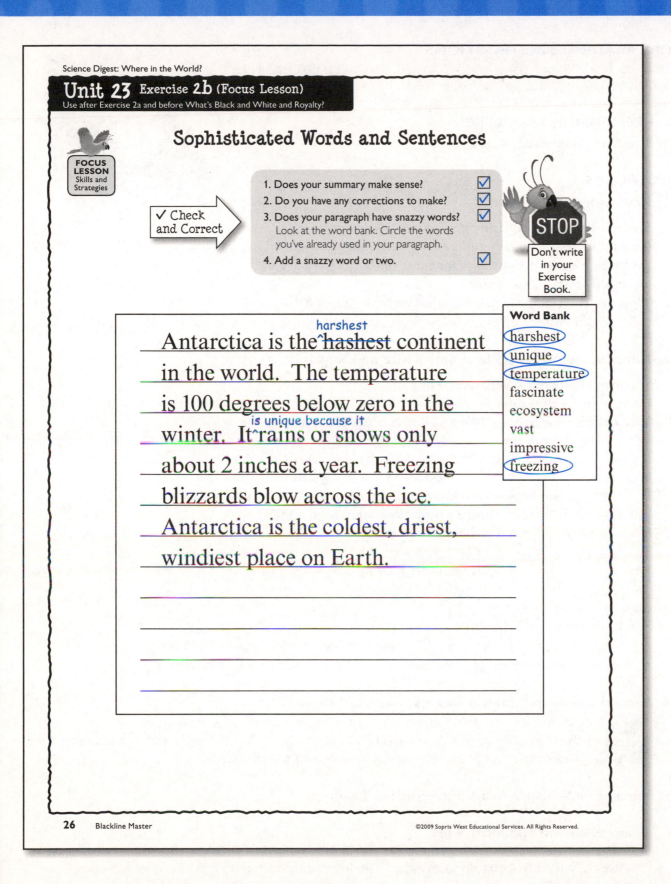

FOCUS LESSON Skills and Strategies

Sophisticated Words and Sentences

✓ Check and Correct

1. Does your summary make sense? ☑
2. Do you have any corrections to make? ☑
3. Does your paragraph have snazzy words? ☑
   Look at the word bank. Circle the words you've already used in your paragraph.
4. Add a snazzy word or two. ☑

STOP Don't write in your Exercise Book.

Word Bank
- harshest
- unique
- temperature
- fascinate
- ecosystem
- vast
- impressive
- freezing

Antarctica is the ^harshest hashest continent in the world. The temperature is 100 degrees below zero in the winter. It ^is unique because it rains or snows only about 2 inches a year. Freezing blizzards blow across the ice. Antarctica is the coldest, driest, windiest place on Earth.

STORY READING 2 INSTRUCTIONS

Students read "What's Black and White and Royalty?" on pages 18–25
and "A Penguin's Calendar" on pages 26 and 27 with the teacher.

COMPREHENSION PROCESSES

Remember, Understand, Apply

PROCEDURES

1. **Reviewing "Antarctica!"**

    Summarizing—Facts; Using Vocabulary—Antarctica
    Quickly review what the students read yesterday. Say something like:
    Yesterday we read about the continent at the bottom of the world.
    What is it called? (Antarctica)
    What are some of the facts we learned yesterday about Antarctica?
    (It's the coldest place on earth. It's a desert. Dinosaurs used to live there . . .)

2. **Introducing "What's Black and White and Royalty?"**

    Viewing; Identifying—What; Inferring
    Have students turn to page 19. Say something like:
    Today we're going to read "What's Black and White and Royalty?"
    We're going to learn about the only animal that can live through the harsh Antarctic winter. First, there
    are a few more clues. Read the riddle. (What's black and white and swims through the sea . . .)
    Look at the pictures. There are two animals that it might be.
    Is it a zebra? (no) How do you know? (A zebra lives in Africa. It doesn't swim in the sea.)
    Is it a penguin? (maybe) Does a penguin swim through the sea? (yes)
    Is it royalty? (maybe) Does it hold its breath? (probably)
    So, our mystery animal might be a penguin.
    Repeat, as appropriate, with the other pictures and then vote.

3. **First Reading**
    *   Ask questions, and discuss the story as indicated by the gray text.
    *   Mixing turns, have students work toward a group accuracy goal of 0–5 errors.
    *   After reading the story, practice any difficult words and reread, as needed.

4. **Second Reading, Timed Readings: Repeated Reading**

    *   As time allows, have students do Timed Readings while others follow along.
    *   Time individuals for 30 seconds and encourage each child to work for a personal best.
    *   Determine words correct per minute. Record student scores.

5. **Partner or Whisper Reading: Repeated Reading**

6. **Comprehension and Skill Work**
    Tell students they will do Comprehension and Skill Activity 2 and Science Digest Entries 2a and
    2b after they read "A Penguin's Calendar." Guide practice, as needed. For teacher directions, see
    pages 50 and 51.

7. **Homework 2: Repeated Reading**

WITH THE TEACHER

18

WHAT'S BLACK AND WHITE AND ROYALTY?

by Ann Watanabe

What's black and white
and swims through the sea?

What's black and white
and royalty?

What's black and white
and holds its breath?

What's black and white,
can you guess?

—Nancy Wing
Read Well 2 Field Test Teacher

19

WITH THE TEACHER

IT'S AN EMPEROR—AN EMPEROR PENGUIN!

An emperor penguin is a bird. Like all other birds, it has feathers. Unlike most birds, the emperor penguin doesn't fly through the air. Instead, it uses its little wings for swimming. This amazing bird can swim about six miles an hour. An emperor penguin spends most of its time in the sea.

FOCUS ON INFERRING

Setting a Purpose

After reading the heading, "It's an Emperor—An Emperor Penguin!" acknowledge student predictions. Say something like:
Wow! The mystery animal is an emperor penguin. It isn't the killer whale. Pat yourself on the back if you guessed right. Isn't that interesting! The only animal that can survive an Antarctic winter is a bird. I wonder how this penguin survives. Let's see if we can find out.

Emperor penguins can swim as deep as 1,800 feet. How deep is that? The deep end of most swimming pools is 10 feet. So 1,800 feet is very deep.

Think about diving down to the deep end of a pool and coming back up 90 times. That's how far an emperor penguin can swim down into the ocean. How would you describe this penguin's swimming abilities?[1]

20

COMPREHENDING AS YOU GO

[1] **Apply:** Inferring; **Understand:** Describing; Using Vocabulary—amazing (An emperor penguin is an amazing swimmer . . .)

Quiz

If you were an emperor penguin, how long do you think you could stay underwater?

a) 22 seconds
b) 22 minutes
c) 22 days

Watch for the answer when you reach page 34.

21

WITH THE TEACHER

WHAT'S WITH THE BLACK AND WHITE TUXEDO?

Emperor penguins look like men dressed up for a fancy party. The penguins aren't dressed up for a party though! The black and white coloring helps protect them. Their black feathers soak up heat from the sun, and their white feathers make it hard for predators to see them in the water.

KEEPING WARM IN THE FREEZING COLD

Emperor penguins need layers and layers of protection to survive the freezing weather.

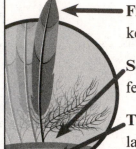

First layer: The penguins' feathers help keep their body heat inside.

Second layer: Under the tightly packed feathers is a layer of air.

Third layer: Under the skin is a thick layer of fat called blubber.

The layers keep the penguin's body heat in and the cold out.

How do emperor penguins survive the freezing weather?1

22

COMPREHENDING AS YOU GO

❶ **Understand:** Summarizing—Facts; Using Vocabulary—survive, freezing (Emperor penguins survive freezing weather because they have three layers to keep them warm. They have feathers, air, and blubber.)

WHAT'S BLACK AND WHITE AND ROYALTY?

FUN FACT

This is a square inch. A penguin may have as many as 70 feathers in this small space.

23

FOCUS ON FACTS AND DRAWING CONCLUSIONS

Identifying—What; Inferring

After reading the fact, say something like:
Wow, that is interesting! How many feathers might the emperor penguin have in that small space? (70) Why is that fact so important to an emperor penguin? (That many feathers in a small space will help keep the penguin warm.)

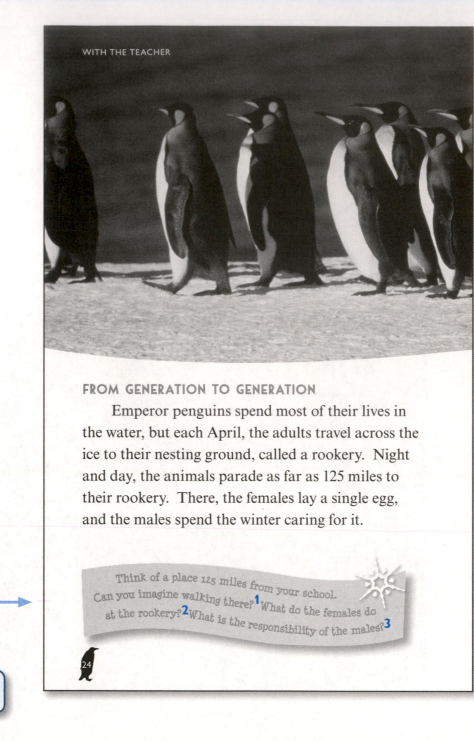

WITH THE TEACHER

FROM GENERATION TO GENERATION

Emperor penguins spend most of their lives in the water, but each April, the adults travel across the ice to their nesting ground, called a rookery. Night and day, the animals parade as far as 125 miles to their rookery. There, the females lay a single egg, and the males spend the winter caring for it.

Think of a place 125 miles from your school. Can you imagine walking there?[1] What do the females do at the rookery?[2] What is the responsibility of the males?[3]

24

COMPREHENDING AS YOU GO

❶ Apply: Making Connections, Visualizing

❷ Remember: Identifying—What (The females lay eggs.)

❸ Apply: Inferring, Explaining; Using Vocabulary—responsibility (The males' responsibility is to care for the eggs.)

WHAT'S BLACK AND WHITE AND ROYALTY?

NESTING

In their nesting ground, the penguins shuffle on the ice to keep warm. The temperature can drop to an unbelievable 125 degrees below zero. No other animal can survive in this cold—only the emperor penguin. As the temperature falls, the penguins huddle in one big group. They take turns standing in the middle where it is the warmest. This way, they protect the eggs and each other.

What is the rookery?**1** How do the males stay warm?**2** Where do you think the females go?**3**

25

COMPREHENDING AS YOU GO

1 Understand: Explaining (The rookery is a nesting ground. It is where penguins lay eggs and take care of them.)

2 Understand: Explaining (They stay warm by huddling together and taking turns being in the middle.)

3 Apply: Inferring (The females go back to the sea. The females go to find food . . .)

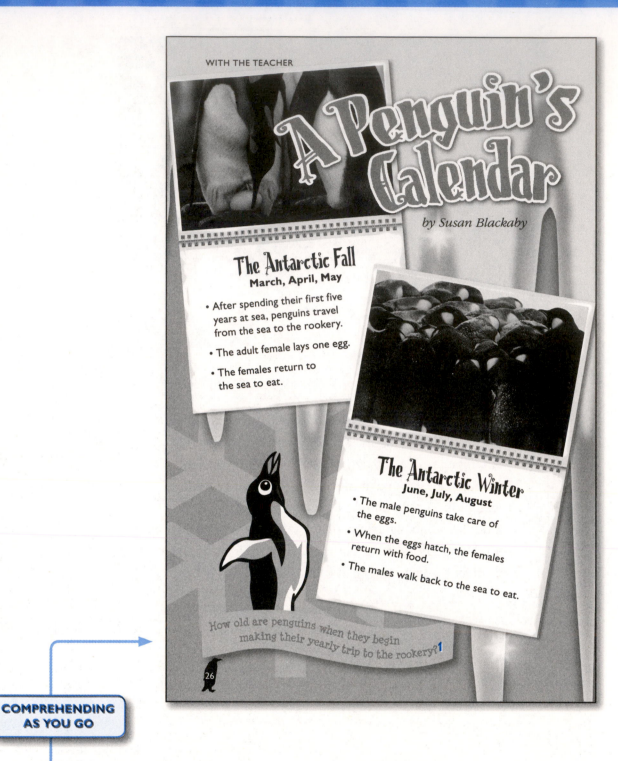

WITH THE TEACHER

A Penguin's Calendar

by Susan Blackaby

The Antarctic Fall
March, April, May

- After spending their first five years at sea, penguins travel from the sea to the rookery.

- The adult female lays one egg.

- The females return to the sea to eat.

The Antarctic Winter
June, July, August

- The male penguins take care of the eggs.

- When the eggs hatch, the females return with food.

- The males walk back to the sea to eat.

How old are penguins when they begin making their yearly trip to the rookery? **1**

26

COMPREHENDING AS YOU GO

1 **Apply:** Inferring (They are five years old.)

48

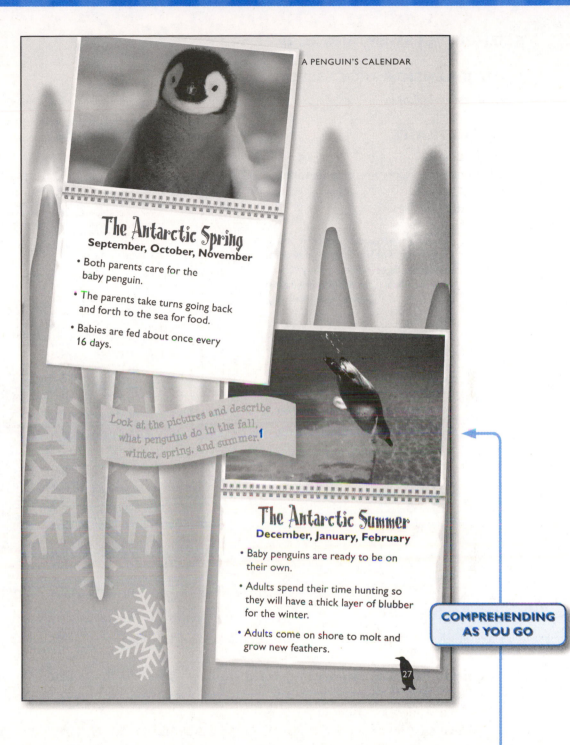

A PENGUIN'S CALENDAR

The Antarctic Spring
September, October, November

- Both parents care for the baby penguin.

- The parents take turns going back and forth to the sea for food.

- Babies are fed about once every 16 days.

Look at the pictures and describe what penguins do in the fall, winter, spring, and summer. **1**

The Antarctic Summer
December, January, February

- Baby penguins are ready to be on their own.

- Adults spend their time hunting so they will have a thick layer of blubber for the winter.

- Adults come on shore to molt and grow new feathers.

27

COMPREHENDING AS YOU GO

❶ Understand: Summarizing, Describing (In the fall, penguins travel to the rookery, where the females lay eggs. In the winter, the male penguins take care of the eggs, while the females go back to the sea. In the spring, the parents take turns going to the sea for food and taking care of the baby penguin. In the summer, penguins fatten up for winter and grow new feathers.)

SCIENCE DIGEST ENTRIES 2a, 2b

COMPREHENSION PROCESSES

Understand, Apply

WRITING TRAITS

Word Choice
Conventions—Complete Sentence,
Capital, Period
Presentation

**Comprehension Monitoring
Using Vocabulary—unique,
temperature, fascinate, ecosystem,
vast, impressive, freezing
Sentence Writing**

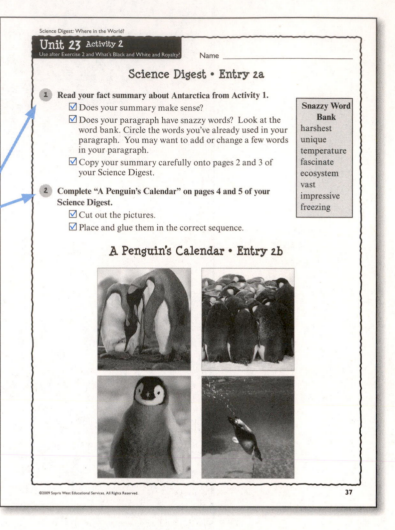

Science Digest: Where in the World?

Unit 23 Activity 2
Use after Exercise 2 and What's Black and White and Royalty!

Name _____

Science Digest • Entry 2a

1. **Read your fact summary about Antarctica from Activity 1.**
   ☑ Does your summary make sense?
   ☑ Does your paragraph have snazzy words? Look at the word bank. Circle the words you've already used in your paragraph. You may want to add or change a few words in your paragraph.
   ☑ Copy your summary carefully onto pages 2 and 3 of your Science Digest.

2. **Complete "A Penguin's Calendar" on pages 4 and 5 of your Science Digest.**
   ☑ Cut out the pictures.
   ☑ Place and glue them in the correct sequence.

Snazzy Word Bank
harshest
unique
temperature
fascinate
ecosystem
vast
impressive
freezing

A Penguin's Calendar • Entry 2b

©2009 Sopris West Educational Services. All Rights Reserved.

37

PROCEDURES

Have students complete the page independently. Guide practice, only as needed.

1. **Comprehension Monitoring, Word Choice—Specific Instructions** (Entry 2a)
   • Have students reread their fact summaries from Activity 1 and decide if they make sense. Have students correct any errors.
   • Have students read the words in the Snazzy Word Bank, then circle any words they've already used in their summary.
   • Have students include additional snazzy words.
   • Have students carefully copy their revised summary onto pages 2 and 3 of their Science Digest.

2. **Sequencing, Following Directions—Specific Instructions** (Entry 2b)
   • Have students cut out the pictures from this activity page.
   • Have students arrange the pictures in the correct sequence, starting with the Antarctic fall.
   • Have students glue the pictures in place on pages 4 and 5 of their Science Digest.

ENTRIES 2a, 2b *(continued)*

Unit 23 Science Digest

Entry 2a

(Accept any reasonable response.)

Antarctica

Antarctica is the harshest continent in the world. The temperature is 100 degrees below zero in the winter. It is unique because it rains or snows only 2 inches a year. Blizzards sweep across the vast ice. Antarctica is

2

Unit 23 Science Digest

the coldest, driest, windiest place on Earth!

3

Unit 23 Science Digest

Entry 2b

Penguins on the March

The Antarctic Fall
March, April, May

Adult penguins march to the rookery. The females lay eggs and return to the sea.

The Antarctic Winter
June, July, August

The males take care of the eggs until they hatch.

Females return with food.

4

Unit 23 Science Digest

Glue the pictures from activity book page 37 into the boxes. See storybook pages 26 and 27 if you need help.

The Antarctic Spring
September, October, November

Both parents take turns going to the sea to eat and taking care of the babies.

The Antarctic Summer
December, January, February

The young penguins and their parents leave the rookery. They go to the sea to hunt.

3-4

5

1 SOUND REVIEW

Use selected Sound Cards from Units 1–19.

2 SHIFTY WORDS

Have students read the words. Use the words in sentences, as needed.

3 ACCURACY AND FLUENCY BUILDING

- For each task, have students say any underlined part, then read the word.
- Set a pace. Then have students read the whole words in each task and column.
- Provide repeated practice, building accuracy first, then fluency.

E1. Tricky Words

- For each Tricky Word, have students use the sounds and word parts they know to silently sound out the word. Use the word in a sentence to help with pronunciation.
- If the word is unfamiliar, tell students the word.

leopards
Look at the first word. The word is *leopards*. Read the word. (leopards)
Large spotted cats found in Africa and Asia are . . . *leopards*.
Read the word three times. (leopards, leopards, leopards)

warning	The kids were told before they came in that the floor was slippery. They were given a . . . *warning*.
figure	We will find a way to solve the problem. We will . . . *figure* . . . it out.
another	J.C. liked the tart apple and asked for . . . *another*.
wondered	"Where did that little bird go?" Jack . . . *wondered*.

- Have students go back and read the whole words in the column.

4 MULTISYLLABIC WORDS

For each word, have students read the syllables, then the whole word. Use the word in a sentence, as appropriate.

petrels	We looked up from our boat, and there flying overhead were . . . *petrels*.
kingdom	The King and Queen were rulers of a large . . . *kingdom*.
successor	The Emperor wanted a . . . *successor*.
recognize	Don put on a disguise so no one would . . . *recognize* . . . him.
parade	We sat along the street waiting for the holiday . . . *parade*.
calendar	Tino checked his schedule on the . . . *calendar*.

5 MORPHOGRAPHS AND AFFIXES

- Have students read the underlined part, then the word.
- Review the morphograph *un-*, as time allows. Say something like:
  Put your finger on the first word. Read the underlined part, then the word. (un, unsettled)
  What does *un-* mean? (not) Right, so unsettled means . . . not settled.

- Repeat practice with whole words, mixing group and individual turns.
  Build accuracy, then fluency.

6 GENERALIZATION: READING NEW WORDS IN PARAGRAPHS

- Have students read the paragraph silently, then out loud. Tell students to use the sounds and word parts they know to read any difficult words.
- Repeat practice, as needed.

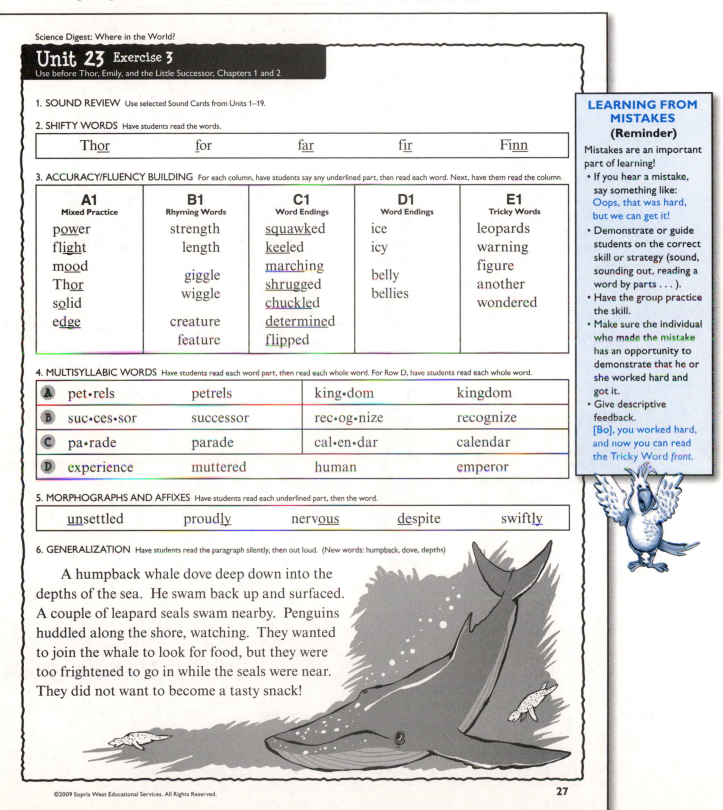

Science Digest: Where in the World?

Unit 23 Exercise 3
Use before Thor, Emily, and the Little Successor, Chapters 1 and 2

1. SOUND REVIEW Use selected Sound Cards from Units 1–19.

2. SHIFTY WORDS Have students read the words.

Thor	for	far	fir	Finn

3. ACCURACY/FLUENCY BUILDING For each column, have students say any underlined part, then read each word. Next, have them read the column.

A1 Mixed Practice	B1 Rhyming Words	C1 Word Endings	D1 Word Endings	E1 Tricky Words
power	strength	squawked	ice	leopards
flight	length	keeled	icy	warning
mood	giggle	marching	belly	figure
Thor	wiggle	shrugged	bellies	another
solid		chuckled		wondered
edge	creature	determined		
	feature	flipped		

4. MULTISYLLABIC WORDS Have students read each word part, then read each whole word. For Row D, have students read each whole word.

A	pet•rels	petrels	king•dom	kingdom
B	suc•ces•sor	successor	rec•og•nize	recognize
C	pa•rade	parade	cal•en•dar	calendar
D	experience	muttered	human	emperor

5. MORPHOGRAPHS AND AFFIXES Have students read each underlined part, then the word.

unsettled	proudly	nervous	despite	swiftly

6. GENERALIZATION Have students read the paragraph silently, then out loud. (New words: humpback, dove, depths)

A humpback whale dove deep down into the depths of the sea. He swam back up and surfaced. A couple of leopard seals swam nearby. Penguins huddled along the shore, watching. They wanted to join the whale to look for food, but they were too frightened to go in while the seals were near. They did not want to become a tasty snack!

LEARNING FROM MISTAKES
(Reminder)

Mistakes are an important part of learning!

- If you hear a mistake, say something like: *Oops, that was hard, but we can get it!*
- Demonstrate or guide students on the correct skill or strategy (sound, sounding out, reading a word by parts . . .).
- Have the group practice the skill.
- Make sure the individual who made the mistake has an opportunity to demonstrate that he or she worked hard and got it.
- Give descriptive feedback. *[Bo], you worked hard, and now you can read the Tricky Word front.*

27

COMPREHENSION PROCESSES

Understand, Apply

PROCEDURES

1. Introducing Vocabulary

> ★ strut, unsettled, despite, recognize ★ keel over, vast, continent

- For each vocabulary word, have students read the word by parts, then read the whole word.
- Read the student-friendly explanations to students as they follow with their fingers. Then have students use the vocabulary word by following the gray text.
- Review and discuss the photo and illustrations.

USING VOCABULARY

WITH THE TEACHER

VOCABULARY POWER! 2

★ strut

When you **strut**, you walk proudly with your head held high and your chest out.

The band leader *strutted* down the street at the front of the parade. What is another way to say "I walked proudly to the front of the class"?[1]

un·set·tled

When someone is a little worried or nervous, he or she may feel **unsettled**.

When the puppy was in the house, the cat was *unsettled*. What makes you feel unsettled?[2]

de·spite

Despite is another way to say "even though."

Anthony tripped and fell flat on his face. Anthony laughed at himself *despite* being embarrassed. What did Anthony do even though he was embarrassed?[3]

★ = New

28

---

❶ **Apply:** Using Vocabulary—strut (I strutted to the front of the class.)

❷ **Apply:** Making Connections; Using Vocabulary—unsettled (Missing school makes me feel unsettled . . .)

❸ **Understand:** Using Vocabulary—embarrassed, despite (He laughed at himself even though he was embarrassed.)

---

2. Now You Try It!
- Read or paraphrase the directions.
- Have students read each word by parts, then read the whole word.
- Have students explain or define the words in their own words. Say something like:

  Read the first word. (vast)

  Now let's pretend that we're going to explain or define the word *vast* to a friend. [Arianna], what would you say?

  Start with "A place that is vast . . . " (A place that is vast is enormous.)

  That's right.

- Have students turn to the appropriate page in the glossary and discuss how their definitions are the same as or different from the glossary's. Your students may like their definitions better.

Note: By defining a word in their own words, students are demonstrating depth of word knowledge. Verbatim responses only demonstrate memorization. Encourage paraphrasing.

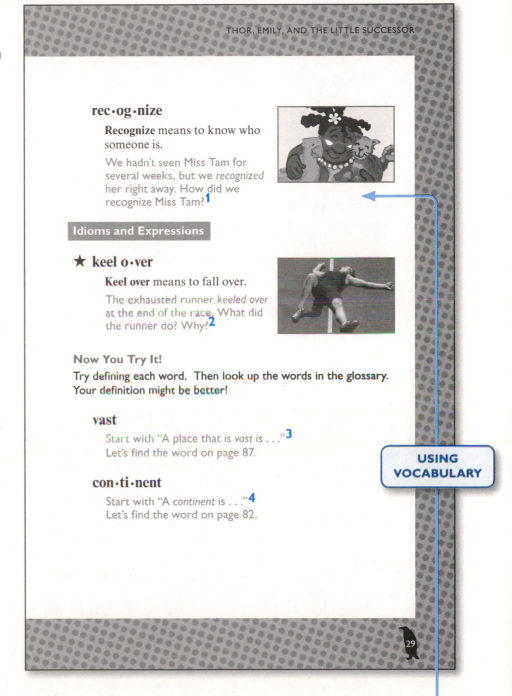

THOR, EMILY, AND THE LITTLE SUCCESSOR

rec·og·nize

Recognize means to know who someone is.

We hadn't seen Miss Tam for several weeks, but we *recognized* her right away. How did we recognize Miss Tam?**1**

Idioms and Expressions

★ **keel o·ver**

Keel over means to fall over.

The exhausted runner *keeled over* at the end of the race. What did the runner do? Why?**2**

Now You Try It!
Try defining each word. Then look up the words in the glossary. Your definition might be better!

vast

Start with "A place that is *vast* is . . ."**3**
Let's find the word on page 87.

con·ti·nent

Start with "A *continent* is . . ."**4**
Let's find the word on page 82.

USING VOCABULARY

29

❶ Apply: Using Vocabulary—recognize (We recognized Miss Tam because we know her well.)

❷ Apply: Inferring; Using Idioms and Expressions and Vocabulary—keel over, exhausted (The runner keeled over. The runner fell over because he was exhausted.)

❸ Understand: Defining and Using Vocabulary—vast; Using Glossary (A place that is vast is very great in size. It is enormous.)

❹ Understand: Defining and Using Vocabulary—continent; Using Glossary (A continent is one of Earth's seven large land areas.)

CHAPTER 1 INSTRUCTIONS

Students read "Thor, Emily, and the Little Successor," Chapter 1 with the teacher and Chapter 2 on their own.

COMPREHENSION PROCESSES

Remember, Understand, Apply

PROCEDURES

1. Reviewing "A Penguin's Calendar"

Summarizing—Facts

Have students turn to pages 26 and 27 and quickly summarize what the emperor penguins do in the fall, winter, spring, and summer.

2. Introducing Chapter 1

CORRECTING DECODING ERRORS

During story reading, gently correct any error, then have students reread the sentence.

Identifying—Title; Inferring—Genre

Discuss the title. Say something like:

What's the title of this story? (Thor, Emily, and the Little Successor)

Do you think this story is fiction or nonfiction? (fiction)

Why do you think that?

(It looks like the main characters are penguins, and they have names.)

Read the chapter title. (It Happens to the Best)

When something happens even to the best, it means it happens to everyone.

3. First Reading

- Ask questions and discuss the story as indicated by the gray text.
- Mix group and individual turns, independent of your voice.
  Have students work toward a group accuracy goal of 0–4 errors.
  Quietly keep track of errors made by all students in the group.
- After reading the story, practice any difficult words.
  Reread the story if students have not reached the accuracy goal.

4. Second Reading, Timed Readings: Repeated Reading

- As time allows, have students do Timed Readings while others follow along.
- Time individuals for 30 seconds and encourage each child to work for a personal best.
- Determine words correct per minute. Record student scores.

WITH THE TEACHER

Thor, Emily, and the Little Successor

by Marilyn Sprick
illustrated by Neal Sharp

Chapter 1
It Happens to the Best

Across the vast Antarctic continent, summer was almost over. In a few months, the land would be wrapped in darkness. Blizzards would cross the land. The Antarctic winter was about to begin. The snow petrels, leopard seals, and humpback whales were leaving for warmer places.

What were the animals doing for the winter? **1**

30

COMPREHENDING
AS YOU GO

1 **Understand:** Explaining (The animals were leaving to spend the winter in warmer places.)

THOR, EMILY, AND THE LITTLE SUCCESSOR

A large emperor penguin named Thor watched as the petrels took flight. "Humph," muttered Thor.

What do you think a petrel is?**1** Why do you think Thor said, "Humph"?**2**

31

COMPREHENDING AS YOU GO

❶ **Apply:** Inferring (A petrel is a kind of bird . . .)
Yes, the book didn't tell you that. You knew they were birds because it said they took flight.

❷ **Apply:** Inferring, Explaining (He said, "Humph," because he wondered what the petrels were doing . . .)

WITH THE TEACHER

Suddenly, a human appeared. Thor had heard about these two-legged creatures. He wasn't frightened. Still, without warning, Thor keeled over onto his back. Shocked at himself, Thor flipped onto his belly and was soon upright again.

"Humph," said Thor.

Describe what happened to Thor. **1** Why do you think he said "Humph" again? **2**

32

COMPREHENDING AS YOU GO

❶ Understand: Describing; Using Idioms and Expressions—keeled over (Thor keeled over onto his back.)

❷ Apply: Inferring, Explaining (He said, "Humph," because he was surprised by what had happened . . .)

THOR, EMILY, AND THE LITTLE SUCCESSOR

"Humph," said Emily with a giggle. "It happens to the best."

Without another word, Thor stood as tall as he could and strutted to the edge of the ice. He dove deep into the chilly ocean waters. Then he swam swiftly down through the icy dark waters.

On land, Emily chuckled.

Who are the main characters?**1**

33

COMPREHENDING AS YOU GO

1 **Understand:** Identifying—Main Characters (The main characters are Thor and Emily.)

WITH THE TEACHER

Down, down, 1,800 feet down in the ocean depths, Thor raced through the water. Speed! Power! Strength! At five years old, Thor was a ruler, an emperor of the sea.

After his shocking experience on land, Thor did not want to surface. He stayed underwater for 22 minutes. Thor thought, "I'll never leave the water again." Still, Thor felt unsettled. Something was odd, but Thor couldn't figure out what it was.

COMPREHENDING AS YOU GO

❶ **Understand:** Identifying—Setting: Using Vocabulary—Antarctica (The story takes place in Antarctica.)

❷ **Understand:** Identifying—Main Characters (The main characters are Thor and Emily.)

❸ **Apply:** Inferring; Explaining; Using Vocabulary—emperor (An emperor is a leader or a ruler.)
   That's right, you learned about emperors in "The Emperor and the Seed."

❹ **Apply:** Predicting; Using Vocabulary—unsettled, survive (He will be captured by a human. He will struggle to survive the winter . . .)

CHAPTER 2 INSTRUCTIONS

Students read Chapter 2 without the teacher, independently or with partners.

COMPREHENSION PROCESSES

Remember, Understand, Apply, Analyze

PROCEDURES FOR READING ON YOUR OWN

1. **Getting Ready**

   Have students turn to Chapter 2 on page 36.

2. **Setting a Purpose**

   Identifying—What; Explaining; Inferring; Drawing Conclusions
   Before students begin reading, say something like:
   As you read the next pages, try to answer these questions:
   - What was Thor doing?
   - Does Thor know where he is going?
   - Think about "A Penguin's Calendar." Is there a clue in the calendar that might tell where Thor is going?

> **PREP NOTE**
> **Setting a Purpose**
> Write questions on a chalkboard, white board, or large piece of paper before working with your small group.

3. **Reading on Your Own: Partner or Whisper Reading**
   - Have students take turns reading every other page with a partner or have students whisper read on their own.
   - Continue having students track each word with their fingers.
   - Have students ask themselves or their partners the gray text questions.

4. **Comprehension and Skill Work**

   For students on an 8-Day Plan, tell them they will do Comprehension and Skill Activities 3 and 4 after they read on their own. Guide practice, as needed. For teacher directions, see pages 67 and 68. (For the 10-Day Plan, see the Lesson Planner, page 9.)

5. **Homework 3: Repeated Reading**

ON YOUR OWN

Chapter 2
Are We There Yet?

The next day, Thor found himself on the solid ice again. He had been determined to swim, hunt, and eat in his icy ocean kingdom. Despite himself, Thor popped up out of the water onto the ice. A parade of older emperor penguins was on the move. Every March, Thor had watched the older penguins leap onto the ice and leave the sea.

36

THOR, EMILY, AND THE LITTLE SUCCESSOR

This year, to his great surprise, Thor found himself marching with the others. Emily joined the parade as well. Thor looked at Emily and said, "Humph," but his feet kept moving.

"Humph," said Emily. Then she said again, "It happens to the best."

Thor said nothing as the winds blew across the ice. He wondered what he was doing. He missed zooming through the deep ocean water, but his feet kept moving—one mile, two miles, three miles. Thor could see nothing but white.

37

Another penguin fell into step with Thor. Thor recognized the other five-year-old, named Finn, but he didn't say anything. "Hey, Thor," squawked Finn. Thor was not in the mood to talk. Finn kept talking anyway. "Are we there yet?" asked Finn.

Thor shrugged and wondered, "Are we where?" Thor didn't say a word, but he knew that he had been here before.

Hours later, Finn squawked again, "Are we there yet?"

Why do you think Finn keeps asking, "Are we there yet?"**1**
Where are Thor and Finn going?**2**

38

COMPREHENDING AS YOU GO

1 **Apply:** Inferring, Explaining (It's a long walk, and he's anxious to get where they're going. He doesn't know where they're going, so he doesn't know if they are there yet.)

2 **Analyze:** Drawing Conclusions (They are going to the rookery.)

MAIN IDEA AND SUPPORTING DETAILS

COMPREHENSION PROCESSES

Remember, Apply

WRITING TRAITS

Conventions—Complete Sentence, Capital, Period
Presentation

Identifying—Topic

Using Graphic Organizer; Identifying—Supporting Details; Inferring—Main Idea; Sentence Writing

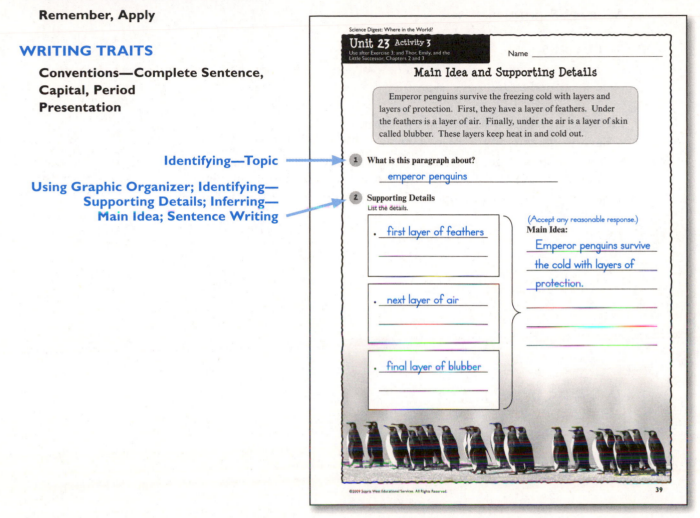

Science Digest: Where in the World?

Unit 23 Activity 3
Use after Exercise 3; and Thor, Emily, and the Little Successor, Chapters 2 and 3

Name _____

Main Idea and Supporting Details

Emperor penguins survive the freezing cold with layers and layers of protection. First, they have a layer of feathers. Under the feathers is a layer of air. Finally, under the air is a layer of skin called blubber. These layers keep heat in and cold out.

1 What is this paragraph about?

emperor penguins

2 Supporting Details
List the details.

- first layer of feathers

- next layer of air

- final layer of blubber

(Accept any reasonable response.)
Main Idea:
Emperor penguins survive the cold with layers of protection.

©2009 Sopris West Educational Services. All Rights Reserved.

39

PROCEDURES

For each step, demonstrate and guide practice, as needed. Then have students complete the page independently.

1. **Topic: Answering Questions—Basic Instructions** (Item 1)
   - Have students read the paragraph in the box.
   - Have students read the question and write the topic in the blank.

2. **Main Idea/Supporting Details: Hierarchy Chart—Basic Instructions** (Item 2)
   - Have students complete the graphic organizer by listing supporting details.
   - Have students write the main idea sentence.
   - Remind students to start with a capital and end with a period.

   Note: The main idea may be constructed in a variety of ways.

PASSAGE READING FLUENCY

FLUENCY

Accuracy, Expression, Rate

PROCEDURES

For each step, demonstrate and guide practice, as needed. Then have students complete the page independently.

Passage Reading—Basic Instructions
- Have students read the practice words.
- Have students finger track and whisper read the story two times—the first time for accuracy and the second time for expression. Have students cross out a lightbulb each time they finish.
- Have students do a one-minute Timed Reading and cross out the timer.

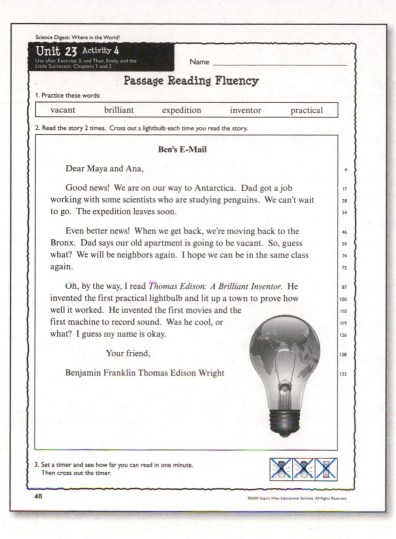

Science Digest: Where in the World?

Unit 23 Activity 4
Use after Exercise 3; and Thor, Emily, and the
Little Successor, Chapters 1 and 2

Name _____

Passage Reading Fluency

1. Practice these words:

vacant	brilliant	expedition	inventor	practical

2. Read the story 2 times. Cross out a lightbulb each time you read the story.

Ben's E-Mail

Dear Maya and Ana,   4

Good news! We are on our way to Antarctica. Dad got a job   17
working with some scientists who are studying penguins. We can't wait   28
to go. The expedition leaves soon.   34

Even better news! When we get back, we're moving back to the   46
Bronx. Dad says our old apartment is going to be vacant. So, guess   59
what? We will be neighbors again. I hope we can be in the same class   74
again.   75

Oh, by the way, I read *Thomas Edison: A Brilliant Inventor*. He   87
invented the first practical lightbulb and lit up a town to prove how   100
well it worked. He invented the first movies and the   110
first machine to record sound. Was he cool, or   119
what? I guess my name is okay.   126

Your friend,   128

Benjamin Franklin Thomas Edison Wright   133

3. Set a timer and see how far you can read in one minute.
   Then cross out the timer.

40

❶ SOUND REVIEW

Use selected Sound Cards from Units 1–19.

❷ SHIFTY WORDS

Have students read the words. Use the words in sentences, as needed.

❸ ACCURACY AND FLUENCY BUILDING

- For each task, have students say any underlined part, then read the word.
- Set a pace. Then have students read the whole words in each task and column.
- Provide repeated practice, building accuracy first, then fluency.

E1. Tricky Words

- For each Tricky Word, have students use the sounds and word parts they know to silently sound out the word. Use the word in a sentence to help with pronunciation.

precious
Look at the first word. Say the word parts silently. Thumbs up when you know the word. Use my sentence to help you pronounce the word.
My pet rabbit is very important to me. It is . . . *precious* . . . to me.
Read the word three times. (precious, precious, precious)

warmth	The people huddled together for . . . *warmth.*
rough	The hike up the snowy mountain was difficult, or . . . *rough.*
worst	The weather is bad, but it's not the . . . *worst* . . . we've had.
zero	Six take away six is . . . *zero.*

- Have students go back and read the whole words in the column.

❹ MULTISYLLABIC WORDS

For each word, have students read the syllables, then the whole word. Use the word in a sentence, as appropriate.

accomplishment	The invention of the automobile was a huge . . . *accomplishment.*
farewell	Another word for goodbye is . . . *farewell.*
tobogganed	Kelsey sledded down the mountain with her friends. They . . . *tobogganed.*
album	We looked at the pictures in our family . . . *album.*
hunker	Tad wants to get out of the wind, so he will . . . *hunker* . . . down behind a rock.
temperature	The aquarium fish do best in water that is just the right . . . *temperature.*

❺ MORPHOGRAPHS AND AFFIXES

- Have students read the underlined part, then the word.
- Repeat practice with whole words, mixing group and individual turns. Build accuracy, then fluency.

❻ GENERALIZATION: READING NEW WORDS IN PARAGRAPHS

- Have students read the paragraph silently, then out loud. Tell students to use the sounds and word parts they know to read any difficult words.
- Repeat practice, as needed.

Science Digest: Where in the World?

Unit 23 Exercise 4a
Use before Thor, Emily, and the Little Successor, Chapters 3 and 4

1. SOUND REVIEW Use selected Sound Cards from Units 1–19.

2. SHIFTY WORDS Have students read the words.

small	call	cell	bell	bellow

3. ACCURACY/FLUENCY BUILDING For each column, have students say any underlined part, then read each word. Next, have them read the column.

A1 Mixed Practice	B1 Names and Places	C1 Word Endings	D1 Word Endings	E1 Tricky Words
known	Emily	swooshing	chicks	precious
photo	Natalie	dropping	females	warmth
harsher	Finn	neared	belly	rough
trek	Antarctic	clicked	bellies	worst
center		checked		zero
blubber		nearer	family	
		trumpeted	families	

4. MULTISYLLABIC WORDS Have students read each word part, then read each whole word. For Row D, have students read each whole word.

A	ac•com•plish•ment	accomplishment	fare•well	farewell
B	to•bog•ganed	tobogganed	al•bum	album
C	hun•ker	hunker	tem•per•a•ture	temperature
D	degrees	rookery	huddled	successors

5. MORPHOGRAPHS AND AFFIXES Have students read the underlined part, then the word.

A	responsibility	instinct	distressed	unprotected
B	uncomfortable	celebration	quietly	joyous

6. GENERALIZATION Have students read the paragraph silently, then out loud. (New words: fluffy, speckled, ever-watchful)

The little speckled penguin huddled between his mom's feet. Then the fluffy little chick waddled away, curiously looking around. Oh, no. He looked around. Where did his mom go? But his ever-watchful mom had an eye on him, and he recognized her coming toward him from among the group of penguins.

BUILDING INDEPENDENCE (Reminder)

Some students will try to follow your voice instead of learning to read the sounds and words. Therefore, it is important for you to demonstrate and guide practice only as needed.

Give students many opportunities to respond without your assistance—with groups and individuals. Encourage independence.

FOCUS LESSON
Skills and Strategies

VOCABULARY LOG

PURPOSE

The purpose of this lesson is to provide explicit instruction in how students can write word definitions in their own words. The lesson prepares students for Comprehension and Skill Work.

PREP NOTES

To demonstrate how to complete a vocabulary log, use an overhead of page 29 in student *Exercise Book 4*, write on a transparency placed over the page, or use a paper copy.

COMPREHENSION PROCESSES

Understand

PROCEDURES

1 INTRODUCTION

Explain the purpose of the lesson. Say something like:

You've done a Vocabulary Log before, but today you are going to define the words in your own words.

When you can define a word in your own words, you are a Vocabulary Master.

PACING

Exercise 4b should take about 10 minutes.

2 CREATING DEFINITIONS AND SENTENCES, USING THE GLOSSARY TO CHECK

Defining and Using Vocabulary—harsh, unsettled; Identifying—Fact; Using Glossary

Everyone, read the words on the Vocabulary Log. (harsh, unsettled)

The log in your focus lesson has two words that describe something or someone.

The words are called adjectives. What are the words called? (adjectives)

When you come up with your own definition for an adjective, you can often start your definition with the word *someone* or *something*. Read the first word. (harsh)

The word *harsh* is often used to describe *something.*

So, we could start our definition with "Something that is . . . "

The story used the word *harsh* to describe Antarctica.

In our own words, we might say "Something that is harsh is very, very hard."

What else could we say? (Something that is harsh is bad. It is difficult.)

Watch me write that.

Under "Definition—In Your Own Words," write "Something that is harsh is very bad or difficult."

Just like we do with "Now You Try It," we can look in the glossary to check our definition.

Everyone, turn in your storybook to the glossary. Find *harsh* on page 83.

What does the glossary say? (Something that is harsh is uncomfortable, difficult, or rough.)

Now read our definition. (Something that is harsh is very bad or difficult.)

I think I like our definition better. Does it tell about Antarctica? (yes)

Next we're going to write our own sentences. Read the sentence in the glossary.

(The pioneers traveled through rain, snowstorms, and other harsh weather.)

The glossary sentence tells about the pioneers' winter weather.

I think it would be nice to use the word *harsh* to describe an event from Thor and Emily's story. I could write, "The winter weather was harsh."

What else might we write? (Emperor penguins are the only animals that can survive in the harsh Antarctic weather . . .)

Those are all great ideas. Remember them for your Vocabulary Log.

Under "Sentence," write "The winter weather was harsh."

Repeat with *unsettled* and the sentence starter "Someone who is . . . "

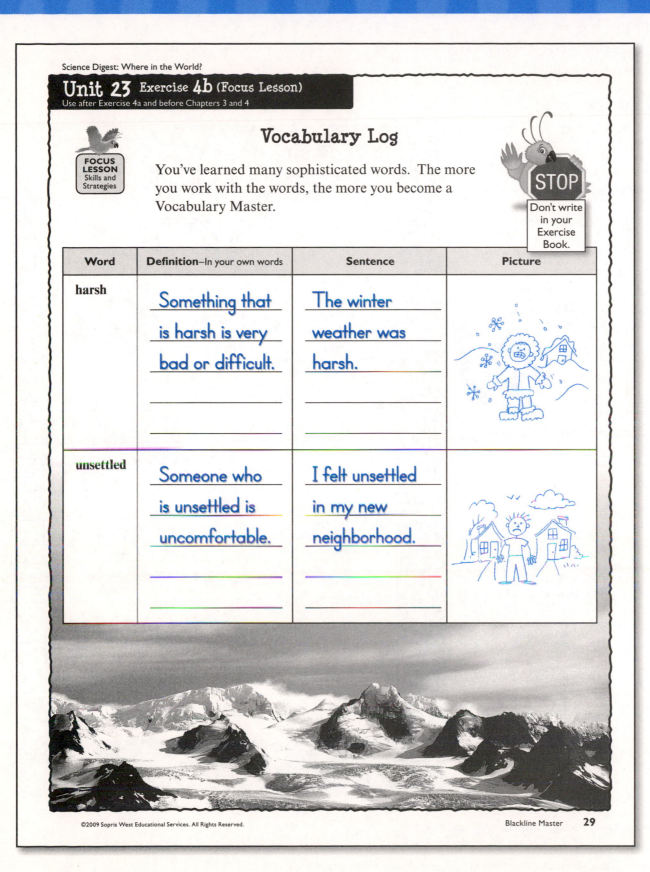

Science Digest: Where in the World?

Unit 23 Exercise **4b** (Focus Lesson)
Use after Exercise 4a and before Chapters 3 and 4

FOCUS LESSON Skills and Strategies

Vocabulary Log

You've learned many sophisticated words. The more you work with the words, the more you become a Vocabulary Master.

STOP Don't write in your Exercise Book.

Word	Definition—In your own words	Sentence	Picture
harsh	Something that is harsh is very bad or difficult.	The winter weather was harsh.	
unsettled	Someone who is unsettled is uncomfortable.	I felt unsettled in my new neighborhood.	

Blackline Master **29**

COMPREHENSION PROCESSES

Understand, Apply

PROCEDURES

1. Introducing Vocabulary

> harsh ★ trek ★ toboggan
> ★ instinct ★ hunker down,
> successor

- For each vocabulary word, have students read the word by parts, then read the whole word.
- Read the student-friendly explanations to students as they follow with their fingers. Then have students use the vocabulary word by following the gray text.
- Review and discuss the photos and illustrations.

USING VOCABULARY

WITH THE TEACHER

VOCABULARY POWER! 3

harsh

Something is **harsh** when it is uncomfortable, difficult, or rough.

The pioneers traveled through rain and snowstorms. The weather was . . . [1]
What made the weather *harsh*? [2]

★ **trek**

A **trek** is a difficult trip or journey.

The explorers left their boats and made the long and difficult journey to the South Pole. What did the explorers go on? [3]

★ **to·bog·gan**

Toboggan means to slide across the snow.

Pam *tobogganed* down the hill on her sled. What did she do? [4]

★ = New

39

---

❶ Understand: Using Vocabulary—harsh (harsh)

❷ Apply: Using Vocabulary—harsh (The weather was uncomfortable and made the trip difficult.)

❸ Apply: Using Vocabulary—trek (The explorers went on a trek.)

❹ Understand: Using Vocabulary—toboggan (Pam slid down the hill on her sled.)

2. Now You Try It!
- Read or paraphrase the directions.
- Have students read the word by parts, then read the whole word.
- Have students explain or define the word in their own words. Say something like:

  Look at the word. Say the parts, then read the whole word.

  (suc•ces•sor, successor)

  Now let's pretend that we're going to explain or define the word *successor* to a friend. [Makayla], what would you say?

  Start with "A *successor* is . . . " (A successor is the person who takes over someone's job.)

  That's right. A successor is the person who takes over someone's job.

- Have students turn to the appropriate page in the glossary and discuss how their definition is the same as or different from the glossary's. Your students may like their definition better.

Note: By defining a word in their own words, students are demonstrating depth of word knowledge. Verbatim responses only demonstrate memorization. Encourage paraphrasing.

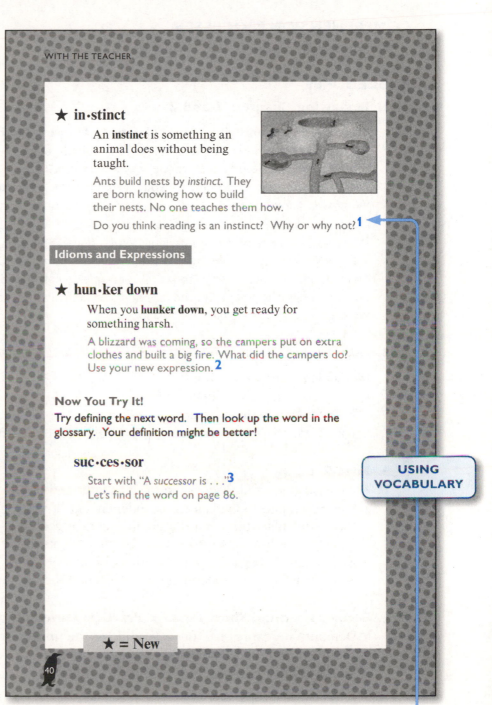

WITH THE TEACHER

★ **in·stinct**

An **instinct** is something an animal does without being taught.

Ants build nests by *instinct*. They are born knowing how to build their nests. No one teaches them how.

Do you think reading is an instinct? Why or why not?[1]

Idioms and Expressions

★ **hun·ker down**

When you **hunker down**, you get ready for something harsh.

A blizzard was coming, so the campers put on extra clothes and built a big fire. What did the campers do? Use your new expression.[2]

Now You Try It!
Try defining the next word. Then look up the word in the glossary. Your definition might be better!

suc·ces·sor

Start with "A *successor* is . . ."[3]
Let's find the word on page 86.

★ = New

40

USING VOCABULARY

❶ **Apply:** Inferring; Using Vocabulary—instinct (Reading is not an instinct because teachers teach us how to read.)

❷ **Apply:** Using Idioms and Expressions—hunker down (The campers hunkered down.)

❸ **Understand:** Defining and Using Vocabulary—successor; Using Glossary (A successor is the person who takes over someone's job.)

CHAPTER 3 INSTRUCTIONS

Students read Chapter 3 with the teacher and Chapter 4 on their own.
Note: If you're working a 10-Day Plan, you will read Chapter 4 with students.

COMPREHENSION PROCESSES

Remember, Understand, Apply, Analyze

PROCEDURES

1. **Reviewing Chapters 1 and 2**

   Summarizing; Identifying—What; Inferring; Drawing Conclusions

   Review the main idea of the story so far. Quickly discuss the questions from Chapter 2, Setting a Purpose. Say something like:

   Yesterday you read Chapter 2 on your own. Let's see what you found out.

   What was Thor doing? (He was marching with the other penguins.)

   Does Thor know where he is going? (no)

   What question does Finn keep asking? Why? (He keeps asking, "Are we there yet?" It's a long march. He's tired and not sure where he's going . . .)

   Think about "A Penguin's Calendar." Is there a clue in the calendar that might tell where Thor is going? (In the fall, emperor penguins walk to their rookery, so maybe Thor is going to the rookery.)

2. **Introducing Chapter 3**

   Identifying—Title; Inferring

   Discuss the title. Say something like:

   What's the title of this chapter? (Almost There!)

   What do you think the title means? (They're almost to the rookery.)

3. **First Reading**
   - Ask questions and discuss the story as indicated by the gray text.
   - Mix group and individual turns, independent of your voice.
     Have students work toward a group accuracy goal of 0–6 errors.
     Quietly keep track of errors made by all students in the group.
   - After reading the story, practice any difficult words.
     Reread the story if students have not reached the accuracy goal.

4. **Second Reading, Short Passage Practice: Developing Prosody**
   - Demonstrate expressive, fluent reading of the first two paragraphs.
   - Guide practice with your voice.
   - Provide individual turns while others track with their fingers and whisper read.
   - Repeat with one paragraph at a time.

THOR, EMILY, AND THE LITTLE SUCCESSOR

Chapter 3
Almost There!

Thor did not like
to walk, but walk he did.
Ten miles, 11 miles, 12 miles,
15 miles, 20 miles, 40 miles.   The
winds grew even harsher, but the penguins
continued their trek. With each mile he walked,
Thor began to feel more and more determined.
Sometimes, he and the others tobogganed on their
stomachs—swooshing across the ice and snow.

What are the penguins doing? **1** Describe their trek. **2**

41

COMPREHENDING
AS YOU GO

❶ Understand: Explaining (The penguins are traveling to the rookery.)

❷ Understand: Describing; Using Vocabulary—trek, harsh (Their trek is a long walk across
the ice. They don't eat on the way. It is cold and harsh.)

WITH THE TEACHER

Finally, as they neared the end of their second day of walking and tobogganing, Thor recognized where he was. He was getting near the rookery where he was born. It was then that Thor answered Finn, "We are almost there."

When Thor and Finn arrived at the rookery, Emily, a penguin named Natalie, and the other females were waiting. Emily said to Thor, "I will lay an egg for us. Our baby will be our successor."

For humans, it was the worst of all weather on Earth. Winds raced across the ice at 120 miles per hour, and the temperature kept dropping—60 degrees below, 65 degrees below, 70 degrees below zero.

But for Emily and Thor and the hundreds of other penguins at the rookery, these were the finest of days. Each emperor female was laying an egg! And each emperor male would be a father. It was a time of great celebration.

What was it like at the rookery?**1** Why was it a time of celebration?**2** What do you think will happen next?**3**

42

COMPREHENDING AS YOU GO

1 **Understand:** Describing (It was like coming home. It was a time to be with family.)

2 **Apply:** Inferring, Explaining (The penguins were laying eggs. They would all soon have baby penguins.)

3 **Apply:** Predicting (The moms will return to the sea to eat. The dads will take care of the eggs . . .)

THOR, EMILY, AND THE LITTLE SUCCESSOR

43

WITH THE TEACHER

Emily laid a beautiful speckled egg. Emily and Thor were very proud! Then carefully, carefully, carefully, Emily passed the egg to Thor. Thor was a little surprised, but then instinct told him that Emily was right. As it had been for every generation of fathers before him, it would be his responsibility to take care of the egg. Thor was brave, strong, and very fat. He could go without food. But Emily was smaller. She would need to return to the sea to eat.

What is an instinct?**1** What was Thor doing that every generation before him had done?**2**

44

COMPREHENDING AS YOU GO

1 Understand: Defining and Using Vocabulary—instinct (An instinct is something an animal does without being taught.)

2 Understand: Explaining; Using Vocabulary—generation (Thor was taking care of their egg, keeping it warm and safe.)

THOR, EMILY, AND THE LITTLE SUCCESSOR

Emily and Thor sang together . . . a sad farewell song. "I will be back. I promise," said Emily. Then she, Natalie, and the other females began their parade back to the sea.

In the never-ending dark of the Antarctic winter, Thor and Finn huddled with the other male penguins in their colony. The fathers had their blubber and each other to keep them warm. Each penguin father had one precious egg on his feet.

Why do you think this might be a bittersweet time for the penguins?**1**
Why did the females leave?**2**

45

COMPREHENDING
AS YOU GO

❶ Apply: Inferring; Using Vocabulary—bittersweet (It is a bittersweet time because they are happy to have an egg, which will hatch into a baby penguin, but it is sad to be apart.)

❷ Understand: Explaining (They had to return to the sea to eat.)

WITH THE TEACHER

One day, the ever-watchful Finn cried, "Oh, no!" At that, Thor looked out from the pack. An egg was rolling out across the ice. Unprotected, the penguin chick inside that egg would not survive—not even for a minute or two. Distressed, Finn said, "Oh, how sad."

Thor said nothing, but he checked on his egg. It was still carefully balanced on his feet. All was well. Finn checked on his egg. All was well. Their eggs were safe and warm. Thor and Finn hunkered down. These eggs would never leave their feet. Never!

Thor and Finn's Questions

ACTION

What do we penguin males do in winter?**1** What do we do by instinct?**2**

CAUSE AND EFFECT

What will happen to our eggs if we drop them on the ice?**3** Do you think the moms will come back?**4**

46

COMPREHENDING AS YOU GO

1 **Understand:** Explaining (Penguin males stay in the rookery and take care of the eggs.)

2 **Understand:** Explaining; Using Vocabulary—instinct (By instinct, male penguins return to the rookery where they were born. They also take care of their eggs by instinct.)

3 **Understand:** Explaining (The eggs will freeze.)

4 **Apply:** Predicting (Yes, they'll come back. They want to help take care of the baby penguins.)

CHAPTER 4 INSTRUCTIONS

Students read Chapter 4 without the teacher, independently or with partners. *Note*: If you're working on a 10-Day Plan, you will read Chapter 4 with students.

COMPREHENSION PROCESSES

Understand, Apply

PROCEDURES FOR READING ON YOUR OWN

1. **Getting Ready**

   Have students turn to Chapter 4 on page 47.

2. **Setting a Purpose**

   Explaining, Inferring

   Before students begin reading, say something like:
   As you read the next pages, try to answer these questions:
   - How long did the father penguins take care of the eggs?
   - How did Thor and Finn feel when their eggs hatched?
   - How did the family members find each other among all the other penguins?
   - What did the mother penguins do?

3. **Reading On Your Own: Partner or Whisper Reading**
   - Have students take turns reading every other page with a partner or have students whisper read on their own.
   - Continue having students track each word with their fingers.
   - Have students ask themselves or their partners the gray text questions.

4. **Comprehension and Skill Work**

   For students on an 8-Day Plan, tell them they will do Comprehension and Skill Activities 5 and 6 after they read on their own. Guide practice, as needed. For teacher directions, see pages 89–91. (For 10-Day Plans, see the Lesson Planner, page 9.)

5. **Homework 4: Repeated Reading**

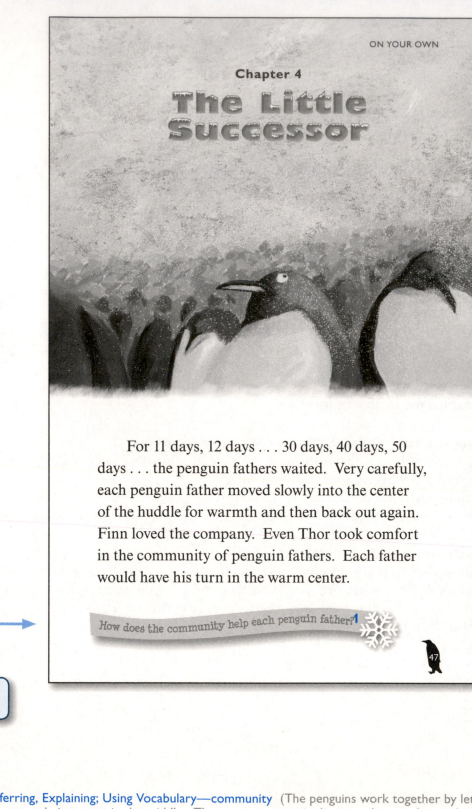

ON YOUR OWN

Chapter 4

The Little Successor

For 11 days, 12 days . . . 30 days, 40 days, 50 days . . . the penguin fathers waited. Very carefully, each penguin father moved slowly into the center of the huddle for warmth and then back out again. Finn loved the company. Even Thor took comfort in the community of penguin fathers. Each father would have his turn in the warm center.

How does the community help each penguin father?[1]

47

COMPREHENDING
AS YOU GO

[1] **Apply:** Inferring, Explaining; Using Vocabulary—community (The penguins work together by letting each father take a turn being warm in the middle. They are a community because they work together. They share the warmth.)

ON YOUR OWN

Then one day, Finn cried, "It's moving!" Nearby, Thor also felt the chick in his egg move. With great pride Thor thought, "Ah, my successor is healthy and strong!"

Three days later, the eggs cracked open. A tiny, wet little chick sat on Thor's feet. Another tiny, wet little chick sat on Finn's feet. In the rookery, there were hundreds and thousands of successors. Thor had never known such a feeling of accomplishment. His chick was fine, and the rookery was a joyous place.

Why was the rookery a joyous place?**1**

48

COMPREHENDING
AS YOU GO

❶ Apply: Inferring, Explaining; Using Vocabulary—generation (The rookery was joyous. It was a happy place because the baby chicks hatched. The penguins would have another generation to take their place.)

THOR, EMILY, AND THE LITTLE SUCCESSOR

But where were the moms? On their way back . . . with bellies full! They were on their way back to the rookery to feed their chicks. Despite himself, Thor trumpeted and Emily heard. Finn trumpeted  and Natalie heard. The moms were close by. Soon Thor, Emily, and their little fluffy gray successor were together again. Finn, Natalie, and their little fluffy gray chick were happy to be a family. All over the rookery, families were meeting and greeting each other.

To his great surprise, Thor whooped and called out, "Life is good!"

Finn just smiled and thought, "Indeed, it is."

49

ON YOUR OWN

Thor bellowed, "I am an emperor, and this is . . . my successor!"

Emily smiled and quietly said, "It happens to the best."

The little penguin successor whistled and clicked.

Why did Thor bellow, "I am an emperor and this is my successor?"[1] This story ended happily. How so?[2]

50

COMPREHENDING
AS YOU GO

❶ **Apply:** Inferring, Explaining; Using Vocabulary—bellow, emperor, successor (Thor bellowed because he was very proud and happy to be a father. He was proud to have a successor.)

❷ **Apply:** Inferring, Explaining; Using Vocabulary—harsh, survive, generation (It ended happily because Thor and Emily's egg survived the harsh winter, and their family would have a new generation.)

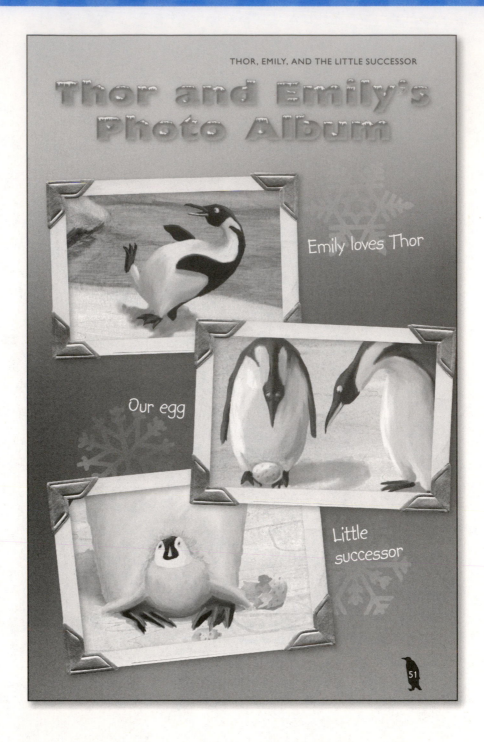

THOR, EMILY, AND THE LITTLE SUCCESSOR

Thor and Emily's Photo Album

Emily loves Thor

Our egg

Little successor

51

VOCABULARY LOG

COMPREHENSION PROCESSES

Understand, Apply

WRITING TRAITS

**Conventions—Complete Sentence,
Capital, Period
Presentation**

**Defining and Using Vocabulary—harsh,
unsettled, vast, unique; Illustrating**

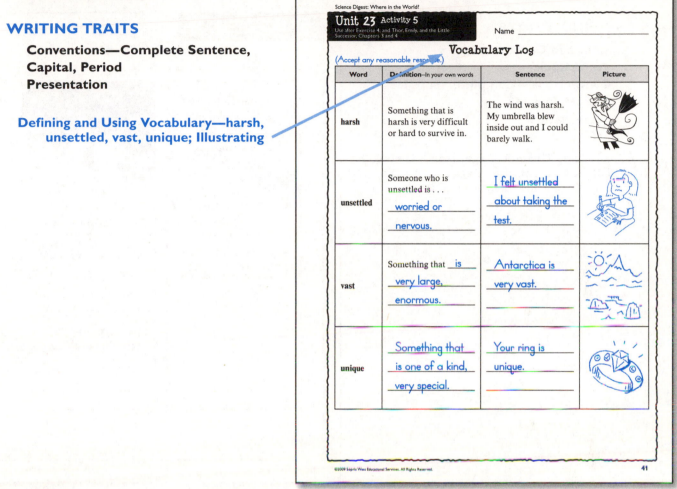

Science Digest: Where in the World?

Unit 23 Activity 5
Use after Exercise 4; and Thor, Emily, and the Little
Successor, Chapters 3 and 4

Name _____

Vocabulary Log
(Accept any reasonable response.)

Word	Definition—In your own words	Sentence	Picture
harsh	Something that is harsh is very difficult or hard to survive in.	The wind was harsh. My umbrella blew inside out and I could barely walk.	
unsettled	Someone who is unsettled is . . . worried or nervous.	I felt unsettled about taking the test.	
vast	Something that is very large, enormous.	Antarctica is very vast.	
unique	Something that is one of a kind, very special.	Your ring is unique.	

©2009 Sopris West Educational Services. All Rights Reserved.   41

PROCEDURES

For each step, demonstrate and guide practice, as needed. Then have students complete the page independently.

Vocabulary: Sentence Writing—Specific Instructions
- Have students read the vocabulary words and write complete-sentence definitions.
- Have students write a sentence using each vocabulary word. Remind them to start with a capital and end with a period.
- Have students draw a picture in the box to illustrate their sentence.

THOR AND EMILY'S CALENDAR

COMPREHENSION PROCESSES

Understand, Create

WRITING TRAITS

Ideas and Content
Word Choice
Conventions—Complete Sentence,
Capital, Period
Presentation

**Using Graphic Organizer, Viewing,
Locating Information, Generating Ideas,
Sentence Completion**

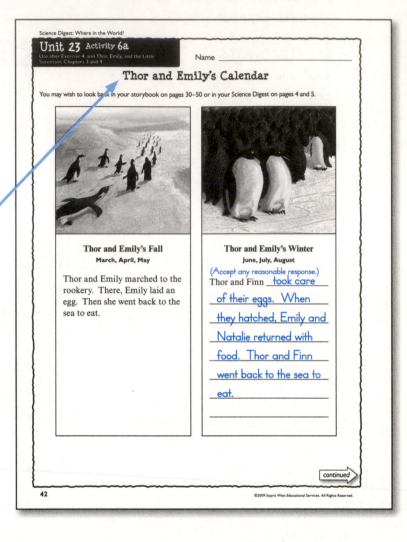

Science Digest: Where in the World?

Unit 23 Activity 6a
Use after Exercise 4: and Thor, Emily, and the Little
Successor, Chapters 3 and 4

Name _____

Thor and Emily's Calendar

You may wish to look back in your storybook on pages 30–50 or in your Science Digest on pages 4 and 5.

Thor and Emily's Fall
March, April, May

Thor and Emily marched to the rookery. There, Emily laid an egg. Then she went back to the sea to eat.

Thor and Emily's Winter
June, July, August
(Accept any reasonable response.)
Thor and Finn _took care of their eggs. When they hatched, Emily and Natalie returned with food. Thor and Finn went back to the sea to eat._

continued

42   ©2009 Sopris West Educational Services. All Rights Reserved.

PROCEDURES

Have students complete the page independently. Guide practice, only as needed.

Calendar: Sequencing, Caption Writing—Specific Instructions

- Have students look at the illustration in the first box (fall) and read the caption.
- Have students look at the picture under the second box (winter), then complete the caption below. Remind them to use capitals and periods.
- Repeat with the other illustration.

THOR AND EMILY'S CALENDAR (continued)

**Using Graphic Organizer, Viewing
Locating Information, Generating Ideas
Sentence Completion**

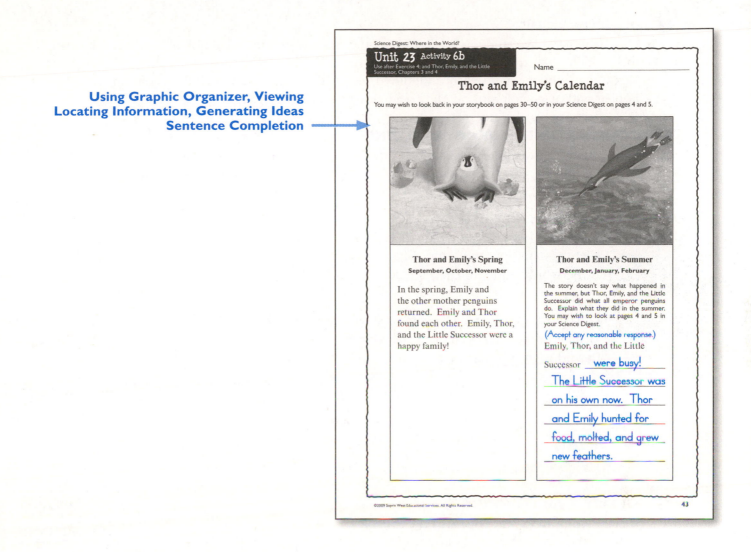

Science Digest: Where in the World?

Unit 23 Activity 6b
Use after Exercise 4; and Thor, Emily, and the Little Successor, Chapters 3 and 4

Name _____

Thor and Emily's Calendar

You may wish to look back in your storybook on pages 30–50 or in your Science Digest on pages 4 and 5.

Thor and Emily's Spring
September, October, November

In the spring, Emily and the other mother penguins returned. Emily and Thor found each other. Emily, Thor, and the Little Successor were a happy family!

Thor and Emily's Summer
December, January, February

The story doesn't say what happened in the summer, but Thor, Emily, and the Little Successor did what all emperor penguins do. Explain what they did in the summer. You may wish to look at pages 4 and 5 in your Science Digest.
(Accept any reasonable response.)
Emily, Thor, and the Little

Successor ___were busy!___
___The Little Successor was___
___on his own now. Thor___
___and Emily hunted for___
___food, molted, and grew___
___new feathers.___

43

91

❶ SOUND REVIEW

Have students read the sounds and key word phrases. Work for accuracy, then fluency.

❷ SOUND PRACTICE

- For each task, have students spell and say the focus sound in the gray bar. For Bossy <u>E</u>, read the header.
- Next, have students read each underlined sound, the word, then the whole column.
- Repeat with each column, building accuracy first, then fluency.

❸ ACCURACY AND FLUENCY BUILDING

- For each task, have students say any underlined part, then read the word.
- Set a pace. Then have students read the whole words in each task and column.
- Provide repeated practice, building accuracy first, then fluency.

E1. Tricky Words

- For each Tricky Word, have students use the sounds and word parts they know to silently sound out the word. Use the word in a sentence to help with pronunciation.
- If the word is unfamiliar, tell students the word.

species
Look at the first word. The word is *species*. Say the word. (species)
Groups of the same kind of animals or plants are . . . *species*.
Read the word three times. (species, species, species)

territory	A dog growls to let others know that his yard is his . . . *territory*.
warmest	Rebecca's mittens were the . . . *warmest*.
above	Do you see the seagulls flying . . . *above*?
among	The deer were hidden . . . *among* . . . the trees.

- Have students go back and read the whole words in the column.

❹ MULTISYLLABIC WORDS

For each word, have students read the syllables, then the whole word. Use the word in a sentence, as appropriate.

tropical	My parents went on vacation to a . . . *tropical* . . . island.
emergent	One of the layers of a rain forest is the . . . *emergent* . . . layer.
understory	One of the layers of a rain forest is the . . . *understory*.
canopy	A roof-like structure or covering is a . . . *canopy*.
eternal	I want our friendship to last. I want it to be . . . *eternal*.
equator	It's warm year-round near the . . . *equator*.

> **MULTISYLLABIC WORDS CORRECTION PROCEDURE**
>
> If students make an error, put the word on the board. Draw loops under each syllable and guide practice with your hand. Have students say each syllable, then read the whole word.

❺ NAMES, PLACES, AND ANIMALS

- Tell students these are people, places, and animals they will read about in the story.
- Have students use the sounds and word parts they know to figure out the words. Use the words in sentences, as needed.

6 MORPHOGRAPHS AND AFFIXES
- Have students read the underlined part, then the whole word.
- Review the morphographs *pre-* and *re-*, as time allows.
- Repeat practice with whole words, mixing group and individual turns. Build accuracy, then fluency.

Science Digest: Where in the World?

Unit 23 Exercise 5
Use before The Tropical Rain Forest, Chapter 1

1. SOUND REVIEW Have students review sounds for accuracy, then for fluency.

A	ea as in bread	ow as in snow	o as in open	oa as in boat	i as in silence
B	aw	ue	kn	oi	ce

2. SOUND PRACTICE In each column, have students spell and say the sound, next say any underlined sound and the word, then read the column.

or	oa	ey	Bossy E
formed	boast	monkey	snakes
forest	coast	money	vines
north	soak	honey	hesitate

3. ACCURACY/FLUENCY BUILDING For each column, have students say any underlined part, then read each word. Next, have them read the column.

A1 Mixed Practice	B1 Word Endings	C1 Rhyming Words	D1 Multisyllabic Words	E1 Tricky Words
damp	collected	cold	umbrellas	species
below	acres	sold	talons	territory
soil	attracts	hold	continents	warmest
rain	wettest	told	monkeys	above
emerge	reaches		decomposers	among
	layers			

4. MULTISYLLABIC WORDS Have students read each word part, then read each whole word.

A	trop·i·cal	tropical	e·mer·gent	emergent
B	un·der·stor·y	understory	can·o·py	canopy
C	e·ter·nal	eternal	e·qua·tor	equator

5. NAMES, PLACES, AND ANIMALS Have students use the sounds and word parts they know to figure out the words.

A	Asia	Sweden	Costa Rica
B	jaguar	tapir (tā·per)	Roland Tiensuu (tee·en·soo)

6. MORPHOGRAPHS AND AFFIXES Have students read the underlined part, then the word.

presoak	brightly	experience	rediscovered

COMPREHENSION PROCESSES

Understand, Apply

PROCEDURES

1. Introducing Vocabulary

> emerge ★ eternal ★ talons ★ rarely ★ territory, equator, predator, hesitate

- For each vocabulary word, have students read the word by parts, then read the whole word.
- Read the student-friendly explanations to students as they follow with their fingers. Then have students use the vocabulary word by following the gray text.
- Review and discuss the photos.

USING VOCABULARY

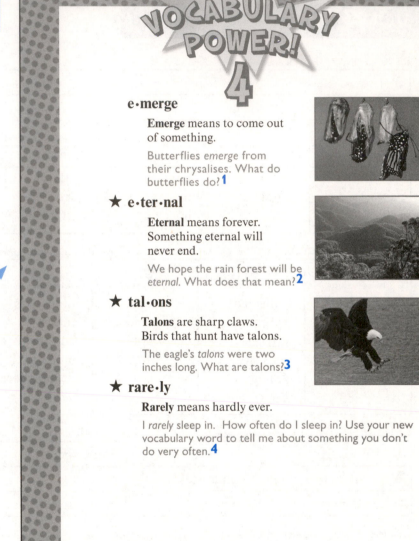

WITH THE TEACHER

VOCABULARY POWER! 4

e·merge

Emerge means to come out of something.

Butterflies *emerge* from their chrysalises. What do butterflies do?[1]

★ e·ter·nal

Eternal means forever. Something eternal will never end.

We hope the rain forest will be *eternal*. What does that mean?[2]

★ tal·ons

Talons are sharp claws. Birds that hunt have talons.

The eagle's *talons* were two inches long. What are talons?[3]

★ rare·ly

Rarely means hardly ever.

I *rarely* sleep in. How often do I sleep in? Use your new vocabulary word to tell me about something you don't do very often.[4]

★ = New

52

---

❶ **Understand:** Using Vocabulary—emerge (Butterflies come out of chrysalises.)

❷ **Apply:** Using Vocabulary—eternal (We hope it will never end. We hope it will be there forever.)

❸ **Understand:** Defining and Using Vocabulary—talons (Talons are sharp claws.)

❹ **Apply:** Using Vocabulary—rarely (You hardly ever sleep in.) (I rarely stay up late.)

2. Now You Try It!

• Read or paraphrase the directions.

• Have students read the words by parts, then read the whole word.

• Have students explain or define the words in their own words. Say something like:

Look at the first word. Say the parts, then read the whole word.

(e•qua•tor, equator)

Now let's pretend that we're going to explain or define the word *equator* to a friend. [Sienna], what would you say?

Start with "The *equator is* . . . " (The equator is a line around the middle of the Earth.)

That's right. The equator is a line around the middle of the Earth.

• Have students turn to the appropriate page in the glossary and discuss how their definition is the same as or different from the glossary's. Your students may like their definition better.

Note: By defining a word in their own words, students are demonstrating depth of word knowledge. Verbatim responses only demonstrate memorization. Encourage paraphrasing.

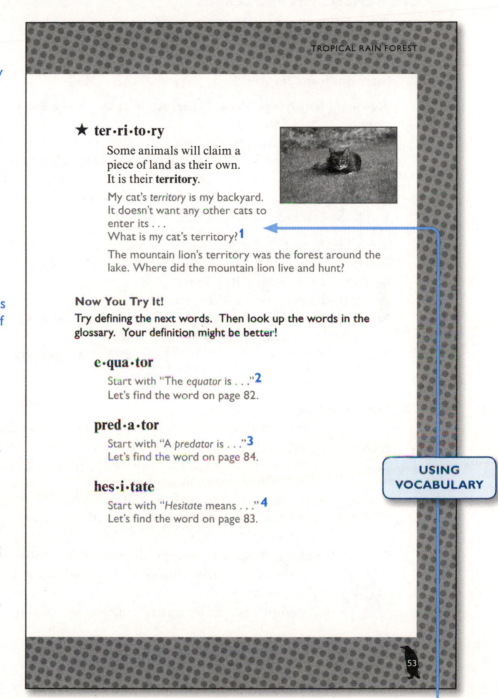

TROPICAL RAIN FOREST

★ **ter·ri·to·ry**

Some animals will claim a piece of land as their own. It is their **territory**.

My cat's *territory* is my backyard. It doesn't want any other cats to enter its . . .
What is my cat's territory? **1**

The mountain lion's territory was the forest around the lake. Where did the mountain lion live and hunt?

Now You Try It!

Try defining the next words. Then look up the words in the glossary. Your definition might be better!

e·qua·tor

Start with "The *equator* is . . ."**2**
Let's find the word on page 82.

pred·a·tor

Start with "A *predator* is . . ."**3**
Let's find the word on page 84.

hes·i·tate

Start with "*Hesitate* means . . ."**4**
Let's find the word on page 83.

USING VOCABULARY

53

❶ Apply: Using Vocabulary—territory (territory; My cat's territory is my backyard.)

❷ Understand: Defining and Using Vocabulary—equator; Using Glossary (The equator is an imaginary line around the middle of the Earth.)

❸ Understand: Defining and Using Vocabulary—predator; Using Glossary (A predator is an animal that hunts other animals for food.)

❹ Understand: Defining and Using Vocabulary—hesitate; Using Glossary (Hesitate means to stop before saying or doing something.)

CHAPTER 1 INSTRUCTIONS
Students read Chapter 1 of "Tropical Rain Forest" with the teacher.

COMPREHENSION PROCESSES
Understand, Apply, Analyze, Evaluate

PROCEDURES

1. **Introducing Chapter 1**

   Viewing; Identifying—What, Title, Author; Using Vocabulary—planet

   Discuss the new story. Say something like:

   Turn to pages 54 and 55. Look at the picture. What do you see?
   (Earth—the blue planet, astronauts, Miss Tam, Scraggly Cat, and Minnie Bird)
   This page gives us another riddle. "Where in the World . . . "
   Touch the first bullet and read. (does it rain almost every day?)

   CORRECTING DECODING ERRORS

   During story reading, gently correct any error, then have students reread the sentence.

   Repeat with each bullet.
   Find the answer. What does it say? (Answer: The rain forests of the world.)
   Read the title. (Tropical Rain Forest)
   Who's the author? (Paula Rich)
   Paula Rich has traveled to many places in the world. Like Miss Tam, Ms. Rich carefully prepares for each trip—saving money, reading, and planning. She has gone scuba diving on the Great Barrier Reef and hiked through the rain forests of Ecuador and Belize. Ms. Rich is a great writer. She has written many stories in *Read Well 2*.

2. **First Reading**
   - Ask questions and discuss the story as indicated by the gray text.
   - Mix group and individual turns, independent of your voice.
     Have students work toward a group accuracy goal of 0–6 errors.
     Quietly keep track of errors made by all students in the group.
   - After reading the story, practice any difficult words.
     Reread the story if students have not reached the accuracy goal.

3. **Second Reading, Timed Readings: Repeated Reading**

   - As time allows, have students do Timed Readings while others follow along.
   - Time individuals for 30 seconds.
   - Determine words correct per minute. Record student scores.

4. **Partner or Whisper Reading: Repeated Reading**
   Before beginning independent work, have students finger track and partner or whisper read.

5. **Comprehension and Skill Work**
   Tell students they will do Comprehension and Skill Activity 7 and Science Digest Entry 3 after they read Chapter 1. Guide practice, as needed. For teacher directions, see pages 102 and 103.

6. **Homework 5: Repeated Reading**

WITH THE TEACHER

Where in the World

- does it rain almost every day?
- do half of the world's species live?
- is it never too cold and never too hot (always just right)?

54

Tropical Rain Forest
by Paula Rich

Answer: The rain forests of the world

55

WITH THE TEACHER

Chapter 1

Layers of the Rain Forest

Wettest Places on Earth

Tropical rain forests are the wettest places on Earth. Rain forests get from 80 inches to 400 inches of rain each year. It may rain two inches in just one hour.

Tropical rain forests grow in the warmest parts of the Earth, around the equator. They are found on the continents of South America, North America, Africa, Asia, and Australia.

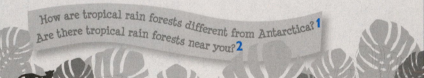

How are tropical rain forests different from Antarctica? **1**
Are there tropical rain forests near you? **2**

56

COMPREHENDING AS YOU GO

❶ Analyze: Contrasting; **Understand:** Using Vocabulary—Antarctica (Tropical rain forests are very wet, and Antarctica is very dry. Rain forests are warm, and Antarctica is very cold. Rain forests have lots of plants and animals, and Antarctica has almost no plants or animals.)

❷ Apply: Making Connections

TROPICAL RAIN FOREST

FUN FACT

It is always warm and wet in a tropical rain forest. In fact, it rains almost every day of the year!

57

The Tropical Rain Forest

Emergent Layer

Tall trees tower above the forest, like umbrellas above a crowd of people. Some trees are more than 200 feet tall. They emerge from the forest.

Canopy

The rain forest canopy is formed by trees that grow from 70 to 100 feet tall. The leaves and branches grow together to form a thick layer.

Understory

The trees of the understory grow about 30 to 50 feet tall.

Forest Floor

There is little plant life on the forest floor, but lots of leaves, fruit, flowers, and animal waste fall from the canopy and understory to the forest floor.

This layer of treetops gets the most light and the most wind. It is not protected from the heavy rain. Birds and bats like to live in this layer.

The treetops of the canopy soak up most of the sunlight. Many plants and vines grow among the trees. Animals have many hiding places in the canopy. Monkeys, birds, snakes, and tree frogs live in this layer.

Below the canopy, the forest is dark, wet, and warm. Plants in the understory grow very slowly because there is so little sunlight. The flowers in this layer are brightly colored and have strong smells to attract insects, birds, and bats.

Little sunlight reaches the forest floor. It is warm, damp, and dark. Decomposers like earthworms recycle the waste to make soil for the trees. Big animals like deer, tapis, and jaguars live on the forest floor.

Describe each layer of the rain forest. **1** If you were an animal, which layer would you want to live in? **2**

58　　　59

1 **Understand: Describing, Summarizing** (The emergent layer has trees that are 200 feet tall. It gets lots of sunlight. The canopy is a thick layer of trees that are 70 to 100 feet tall. Lots of animals live in the canopy. The understory is dark and wet. Plants get little sunlight and grow slowly. The forest floor is dark and damp. Some big animals like jaguars live there as well as some small animals like worms.)

2 **Evaluate: Responding** (I would like to be a harpy eagle and live in the emergent layer where there's lots of sun . . .)

WITH THE TEACHER

Children's Eternal Rain Forest of Costa Rica

Rain forests are a treasure to people all over the world, but many of the forests are being cut down. In 1987, a nine-year-old boy from Sweden decided he wanted to do something. But what?

Roland Tiensuu (Tee-en-soo) decided it would be a great idea to buy and protect a small piece of the rain forest. Roland's teacher and his class helped him earn money. Soon other children heard about Roland's idea. They all wanted to help. The children collected bottles and cans. They sold cookies. Some kids even asked for money for their birthdays so they could help buy some land in the rain forest.

All the money that the children earned and saved went to a group of people who lived in Costa Rica. They bought a little bit of the rain forest. This rain forest is called the Children's Eternal Rain Forest. It's eternal because it will never be cut down. It will be a rain forest forever!

At first, the Children's Eternal Rain Forest was only 15 acres. Children all over the world heard about it and sent money. The park grew and is still growing.

60

TROPICAL RAIN FOREST

In 20 years, the Children's Eternal Rain Forest grew to cover 54,000 acres.

61

After Reading Page 60

1 **Understand:** Describing, Summarizing
What was Roland Tiensuu's plan for saving a piece of the rain forest?
(His plan was to buy a piece of the rain forest.)

2 **Analyze:** Drawing Conclusions; **Apply:**
Using Vocabulary—exceptional
Why was Roland's plan exceptional?
(Roland was only nine when he came up with the plan. His plan worked. There are 54,000 acres of land in the Children's Eternal Rain Forest. Children all over the world have earned money for the rain forest.)

3 **Analyze:** Drawing Conclusions; **Apply:**
Using Vocabulary—eternal
Why is the land called the Children's Eternal Rain Forest?
(It belongs to the children. The word *eternal* means forever. The children hope the rain forest will last forever.)

PASSAGE COMPREHENSION

COMPREHENSION PROCESSES
Understand, Apply

WRITING TRAITS
Conventions—Capital

Identifying—What

Using Graphic Organizer; Inferring—
Facts; Using Vocabulary—
equator, Africa

Using Graphic Organizer
Identifying—Facts

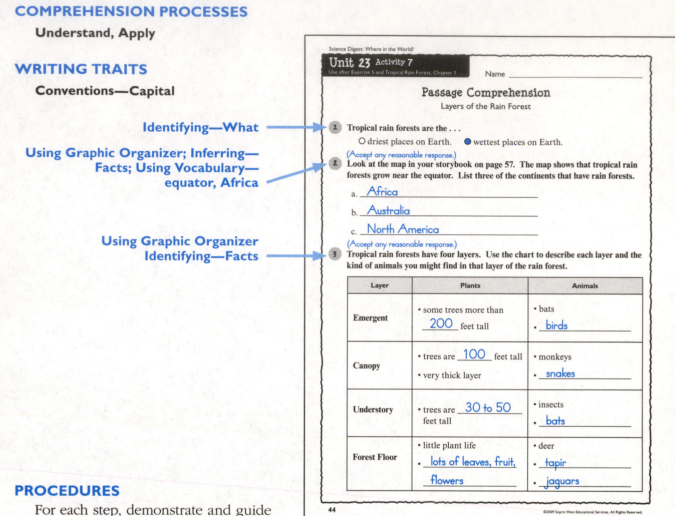

Science Digest: Where in the World?

Unit 23 Activity 7
Use after Exercise 5 and Tropical Rain Forest, Chapter 1

Name _____

Passage Comprehension
Layers of the Rain Forest

1. Tropical rain forests are the . . .
   ○ driest places on Earth.   ● wettest places on Earth.
   (Accept any reasonable response.)

2. Look at the map in your storybook on page 57. The map shows that tropical rain forests grow near the equator. List three of the continents that have rain forests.
   a. _Africa_
   b. _Australia_
   c. _North America_
   (Accept any reasonable response.)

3. Tropical rain forests have four layers. Use the chart to describe each layer and the kind of animals you might find in that layer of the rain forest.

Layer	Plants	Animals
Emergent	• some trees more than _200_ feet tall	• bats • _birds_
Canopy	• trees are _100_ feet tall • very thick layer	• monkeys • _snakes_
Understory	• trees are _30 to 50_ feet tall	• insects • _bats_
Forest Floor	• little plant life • _lots of leaves, fruit, flowers_	• deer • _tapir_ • _jaguars_

44

©2009 Sopris West Educational Services. All Rights Reserved.

PROCEDURES
For each step, demonstrate and guide practice, as needed. Then have students complete the page independently.

1. **Selection Response—Basic Instructions** (Item 1)
   Have students read the sentence starter, then fill in the bubble with the correct answer.

2. **Map: Making Lists—Specific Instructions** (Item 2)
   Have students look at the map on page 57 and find the equator, then list three continents that have land areas near the equator. Say something like:
   Look at the map on page 57 and find the equator. Trace your finger along the equator. We know that rain forests grow near the equator. What continents have land near the equator?
   (North America, South America, Africa, Australia, Asia)
   So those continents have rain forests. Write three of those continents in the blanks. Remember to use capitals for the names of the continents.

3. **Chart: Locating Information—Specific Instructions** (Item 3)
   Have students read the paragraph, then fill in the blanks with the correct answers.

Self-monitoring
Have students check and correct their work.

ENTRY 3

COMPREHENSION PROCESSES

Understand

WRITING TRAITS

Conventions—Complete Sentence, Capital, Period Presentation

Using Graphic Organizer Identifying—What Verifying

Summarizing—Facts

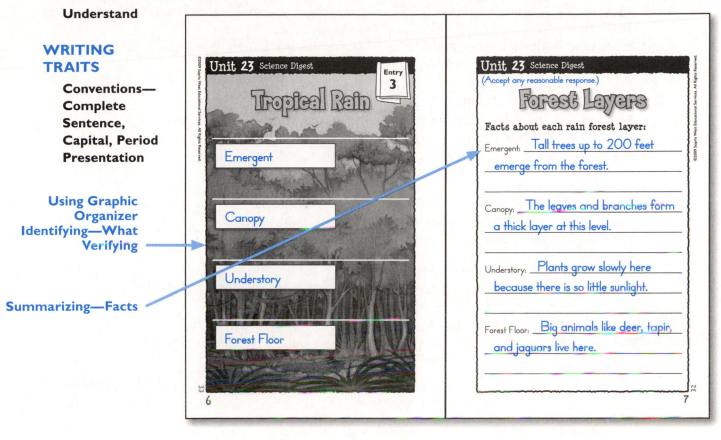

PROCEDURES

For each step, demonstrate and guide practice, as needed. Then have students complete the page independently.

1. **Diagram: Labeling—Specific Instructions**
   Have students label the diagram with the correct rain forest layer. Have students look in the magazine on page 58 to make sure they've done it correctly.

2. **Fact Summary: Sentence Writing—Specific Instructions**
   Have students write a fact about each layer of the rain forest. Remind them to start sentences with a capital and end with a period.

❶ SOUND REVIEW

❷ SOUND PRACTICE
- For each task, have students spell and say the focus sound in the gray bar. For Bossy <u>E</u>, read the header.
- Next, have students read each underlined sound, the word, then the whole column.
- Repeat with each column, building accuracy first, then fluency.

❸ ACCURACY AND FLUENCY BUILDING
- For each task, have students say any underlined part, then read the word.
- Set a pace. Then have students read the whole words in each task and column.
- Provide repeated practice, building accuracy first, then fluency.

C1. Multisyllabic Words
- For the list of words divided by syllables, have students read each syllable, then the whole word. Use the word in a sentence, as appropriate.
- For the list of whole words, build accuracy and then fluency.

suction	A vacuum cleaner has a lot of . . . *suction.*
secretive	Bridgette wouldn't tell what was in her backpack. She was being . . . *secretive.*
canopy	The sun was hot, so I sat under the . . . *canopy.*
mantled	Some monkeys are called . . . *mantled* . . . howler monkeys.
emergent	The top layer of a rain forest is the . . . *emergent* . . . layer.

D1. Tricky Words
- For each Tricky Word, have students use the sounds and word parts they know to silently sound out the word. Use the word in a sentence to help with pronunciation.

toucan

Look at the first word. Say the word parts silently. Thumbs up when you know the word. Use my sentence to help you pronounce the word. One kind of brightly colored bird is a . . . *toucan.* Read the word two times. (toucan, toucan)

weigh	How much does an elephant . . . *weigh?*
territory	A dog growls to let others know that his yard is his . . . *territory.*
searching	I couldn't find my lost dog, but I kept on . . . *searching.*

- Have students go back and read the whole words in the column.

❹ WORDS IN CONTEXT
For each word, have students use the sounds and word parts they know to silently sound out the word. Then have students read the sentence. Assist, as needed.

❺ ANIMALS
- Tell students these are animals they will read about in the story.
- Have students use the sounds and word parts they know to figure out the words. Use the words in sentences, as needed.

❻ MORPHOGRAPHS AND AFFIXES

❼ GENERALIZATION: READING NEW WORDS IN PARAGRAPHS

- Have students read the paragraph silently, then out loud. Tell students to use the sounds and word parts they know to read any difficult words.
- Repeat practice, as needed.

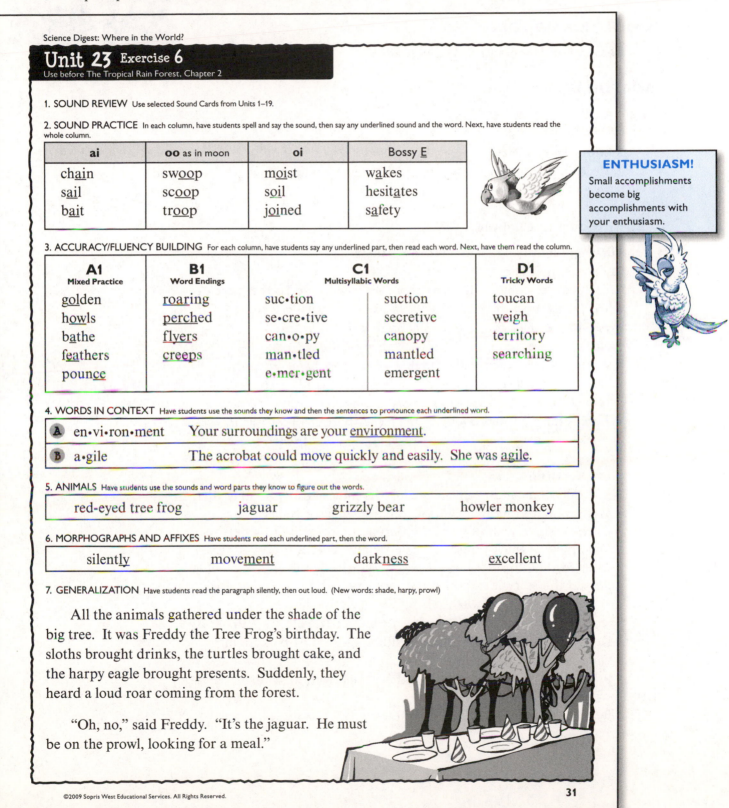

Science Digest: Where in the World?

Unit 23 Exercise 6
Use before The Tropical Rain Forest, Chapter 2

1. SOUND REVIEW Use selected Sound Cards from Units 1–19.

2. SOUND PRACTICE In each column, have students spell and say the sound, then say any underlined sound and the word. Next, have students read the whole column.

ai	oo as in moon	oi	Bossy E
ch<u>ai</u>n	sw<u>oo</u>p	m<u>oi</u>st	w<u>a</u>k<u>e</u>s
s<u>ai</u>l	sc<u>oo</u>p	s<u>oi</u>l	hesit<u>a</u>t<u>e</u>s
b<u>ai</u>t	tr<u>oo</u>p	<u>j</u>oined	saf<u>e</u>ty

ENTHUSIASM!
Small accomplishments become big accomplishments with your enthusiasm.

3. ACCURACY/FLUENCY BUILDING For each column, have students say any underlined part, then read each word. Next, have them read the column.

A1 Mixed Practice	B1 Word Endings	C1 Multisyllabic Words		D1 Tricky Words
gold<u>e</u>n	<u>roar</u>ing	suc•tion	suction	toucan
h<u>ow</u>ls	<u>perch</u>ed	se•cre•tive	secretive	weigh
b<u>a</u>th<u>e</u>	<u>fly</u>ers	can•o•py	canopy	territory
f<u>ea</u>thers	<u>creep</u>s	man•tled	mantled	searching
poun<u>ce</u>		e•mer•gent	emergent	

4. WORDS IN CONTEXT Have students use the sounds they know and then the sentences to pronounce each underlined word.

Ⓐ en•vi•ron•ment   Your surroundings are your <u>environment</u>.

Ⓑ a•gile   The acrobat could move quickly and easily. She was <u>agile</u>.

5. ANIMALS Have students use the sounds and word parts they know to figure out the words.

red-eyed tree frog	jaguar	grizzly bear	howler monkey

6. MORPHOGRAPHS AND AFFIXES Have students read each underlined part, then the word.

silent<u>ly</u>	move<u>ment</u>	dark<u>ness</u>	<u>ex</u>cellent

7. GENERALIZATION Have students read the paragraph silently, then out loud. (New words: shade, harpy, prowl)

All the animals gathered under the shade of the big tree. It was Freddy the Tree Frog's birthday. The sloths brought drinks, the turtles brought cake, and the harpy eagle brought presents. Suddenly, they heard a loud roar coming from the forest.

"Oh, no," said Freddy. "It's the jaguar. He must be on the prowl, looking for a meal."

31

CHAPTER 2 INSTRUCTIONS

Students read pages 62–65 with the teacher and pages 66–69 on their own. *Note*: If you're working on a 10-Day Plan, you will read pages 66–69 with students.

COMPREHENSION PROCESSES

Remember, Understand, Apply, Analyze

PROCEDURES

1. **Reviewing Chapter 1**

   Summarizing—Facts
   Turn to page 56. Have students quickly review what they have learned so far about rain forests.

2. **Introducing Chapter 2**

   Viewing; Identifying—Title, Heading; Inferring
   Say something like:
   We're going to continue learning about the rain forest. Look at page 62.
   What's the title of this chapter? (Animals of the Rain Forest)
   What do you think this chapter will be about?
   (It will be about the animals that live in the rain forest.)
   Read the two headings under the title. (Emergent Layer, Harpy Eagle)
   What do they tell you about what we're going to read next?
   (We're going to read about an animal that lives in the emergent layer.)
   Where is the emergent layer—at the top or bottom of the rain forest? (It's at the top. The harpy eagle must live high in the treetops.)

3. **First Reading**
   • Ask questions and discuss the story as indicated by the gray text.
   • Mix group and individual turns, independent of your voice.
     Have students work toward a group accuracy goal of 0–5 errors.
     Quietly keep track of errors made by all students in the group.
   • After reading the story, practice any difficult words.
     Reread the story if students have not reached the accuracy goal.

4. **Second Reading, Short Passage Practice: Developing Prosody**
   • Demonstrate expressive, fluent reading of the first paragraph.
   • Guide practice with your voice.
   • Provide individual turns while others track with their fingers and whisper read.
   • Repeat with one paragraph at a time.

WITH THE TEACHER

Chapter 2

Animals of the Rain Forest

Emergent Layer

Harpy Eagle

In the towering treetops of the rain forest, harpy eagles rule. These large carnivores are at the top of the rain forest food chain. They perch silently in the trees, watching and waiting for a good meal to pass by.

62

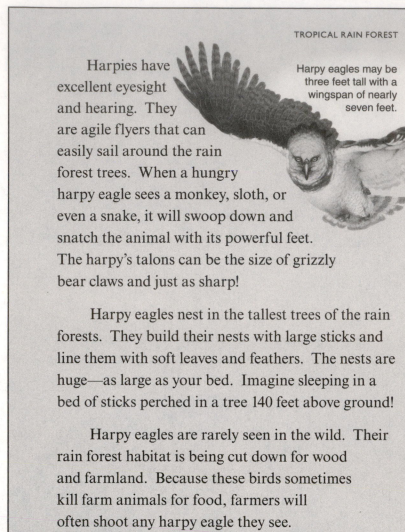

TROPICAL RAIN FOREST

Harpies have excellent eyesight and hearing. They are agile flyers that can easily sail around the rain forest trees. When a hungry harpy eagle sees a monkey, sloth, or even a snake, it will swoop down and snatch the animal with its powerful feet. The harpy's talons can be the size of grizzly bear claws and just as sharp!

Harpy eagles may be three feet tall with a wingspan of nearly seven feet.

Harpy eagles nest in the tallest trees of the rain forests. They build their nests with large sticks and line them with soft leaves and feathers. The nests are huge—as large as your bed. Imagine sleeping in a bed of sticks perched in a tree 140 feet above ground!

Harpy eagles are rarely seen in the wild. Their rain forest habitat is being cut down for wood and farmland. Because these birds sometimes kill farm animals for food, farmers will often shoot any harpy eagle they see.

Describe a harpy eagle.**1**
Why do you think harpy eagles might be endangered?**2**

63

COMPREHENDING AS YOU GO

❶ Understand: Describing; Summarizing; Using Vocabulary—carnivore, prey, talons (A harpy eagle can be three feet tall with a wingspan of seven feet. A harpy eagle is a carnivore. It catches its prey with sharp talons. Harpy eagles have excellent eyesight and hearing . . .)

❷ Analyze: Drawing Conclusions; **Apply:** Using Vocabulary—endangered, habitat (Harpy eagles might be endangered because their habitat is being cut down. Farmers shoot the eagles because they sometimes kill farm animals . . .)

Canopy

Howler Monkey

Howler monkeys live in the trees of the rain forest canopy. They rarely visit the forest floor. Howler monkeys use their long strong tails as an extra arm while climbing and walking through the trees. These monkeys often hang from a branch by their tail, so they can use both hands for eating. They spend the day resting or searching for tasty leaves, fruits, and flowers to eat. At night, they sleep in the trees.

64

TROPICAL RAIN FOREST

With a name like howler monkey, do you think these animals are quiet? No. Their deep, roaring howls can be heard three miles away! Groups of monkeys are called troops. Howler monkey troops howl every day at dawn and at dusk. Each troop is saying, "This is our territory! The food here belongs to us. Stay away!"

Mantled howler monkeys live in Costa Rica. They are between two and four feet tall and have short black fur with long golden hair along their sides.

Describe a howler monkey. **1** What would an ordinary day be like in the life of a howler monkey? **2**

65

COMPREHENDING AS YOU GO

❶ Understand: Describing; Summarizing (A howler monkey lives in the rain forest canopy. It even sleeps in the trees. The howler monkey uses its long tail to hang from branches. It eats leaves, fruits, and flowers . . .)

❷ Understand: Summarizing, Sequencing; Using Vocabulary—ordinary (A howler monkey wakes up at dawn and howls with the rest of its troop. Then the monkey searches for leaves, fruits, and flowers to eat. Sometimes during the day, the monkey rests. Then at dusk, the monkey howls again with its troop. Finally, the howler monkey goes to sleep in the trees.)

CHAPTER 2 INSTRUCTIONS

Students read Chapter 2, pages 66–69, without the teacher, independently or with partners.

Note: If you're working on a 10-Day Plan, you will read pages 66–69 with students.

COMPREHENSION PROCESSES

Remember, Understand, Apply, Analyze

PROCEDURES FOR READING ON YOUR OWN

1. Getting Ready

Have students turn to Chapter 2 on page 66.

2. Setting a Purpose

Explaining; Identifying—What; Contrasting

Before students begin reading, say something like:

> As you read the next pages, try to answer these questions:
> - How do red-eyed tree frogs hold on to the trees?
> - How do the red-eyed tree frogs protect themselves from predators?
> - What do jaguars eat?
> - How is a jaguar different from most other cats?

PREP NOTE

Setting a Purpose

Write questions on a chalkboard, white board, or large piece of paper before working with your small group.

3. Reading on Your Own: Partner or Whisper Reading

- Have students take turns reading every other page with a partner or have students whisper read on their own.
- Continue having students track each word with their fingers.
- Have students ask themselves or their partners the gray text questions.

4. Comprehension and Skill Work

For students on an 8-Day Plan, tell them they will do Comprehension and Skill Activity 8 and their Science Digest Entry 4 after they read on their own. Guide practice, as needed. For teacher directions, see pages 116 and 117. (For 10-Day Plans, see the Lesson Planner, page 9.)

5. Homework 6: Repeated Reading

ON YOUR OWN

Understory

Red-Eyed Tree Frog

In the shade of the understory, a toucan quietly creeps along a branch toward its prey. The toucan is looking very carefully for food. It almost misses the small bright green frog sleeping in the green leaves.

Suddenly, the sleeping frog senses the bird and

66

TROPICAL RAIN FOREST

wakes, opening its huge eyes. The bright red eyes surprise the toucan. The toucan hesitates. In that split second, the frog uses its strong back legs to leap to safety. Blue and yellow stripes on the frog's legs flash as it jumps. The bird is confused by the quick movement and color. The frog is gone before the toucan knows what has happened.

The toucan has just missed having a red-eyed tree frog for lunch. These frogs have suction cups on their toes that help them hold onto tree branches. Red-eyed tree frogs are about two or three inches long. They live in the warm, moist environment of the rain forest understory. They eat insects at night and sleep during the day. As you learned, their big red eyes and colorful legs help protect them from predators.

Describe a red-eyed tree frog. **1**

The red-eyed tree frog lives in the understory of the Costa Rican rain forest.

67

COMPREHENDING AS YOU GO

1 **Understand:** Describing; Summarizing (A red-eyed tree frog lives in the understory. Toucans eat tree frogs. The tree frog's bright red eyes surprise their enemies. The frogs have suction cups on their toes. The frogs are two to three inches long . . .)

ON YOUR OWN

Forest Floor

Jaguar

In the darkness of the rain forest floor, a big spotted cat prowls. Eight feet long from its nose to the tip of its tail, a jaguar can weigh 250 pounds. They can have tan fur with black spots or black fur with black spots.

Jaguars live and hunt in the rain forests of Costa Rica.

68

TROPICAL RAIN FOREST

These huge carnivores will eat almost any animal they can catch—snakes, monkeys, deer, turtles, or frogs. They spend most of their time on the forest floor, but sometimes they will climb a tree and pounce on their prey from above.

Unlike most cats, jaguars like the water. They swim, bathe, and play in streams and pools. They will even catch fish. Some people say a jaguar will use its long tail as fish bait. It waves its tail over the water or taps the water's surface with its tail. A hungry fish might think the jaguar's tail is food and come for a meal. Then the jaguar will quickly scoop up the fish with a big paw.

Scientists believe there may not be many jaguars left in the rain forests. It is hard to know how many jaguars there are because they are secretive animals. Jaguars usually live alone. They hunt mostly at night, so they are not often seen during the day.

Describe a jaguar. **1** What makes a jaguar a successful predator? **2**

69

COMPREHENDING AS YOU GO

❶ Understand: Describing; Summarizing; Using Vocabulary—carnivore (A jaguar is a big cat that weighs 250 pounds. A jaguar can have tan fur with black spots or black fur with black spots. A jaguar is a carnivore. It will eat almost any animal it can catch. Jaguars like water and can even catch fish . . .)

❷ Analyze: Drawing Conclusions; Apply: Using Vocabulary—predator, prey (A jaguar is a successful predator because it hunts at night so its prey can't see it coming. A jaguar can climb a tree to pounce on prey from above. Sometimes a jaguar can trick a fish into thinking that its tail is food . . .)

PASSAGE COMPREHENSION • RAIN FOREST ANIMALS

COMPREHENSION PROCESSES
Understand

WRITING TRAITS
Conventions—Complete Sentence, Capital, Period
Presentation

Identifying—Facts; Test Taking

Viewing; Explaining—Facts
Sentence Writing

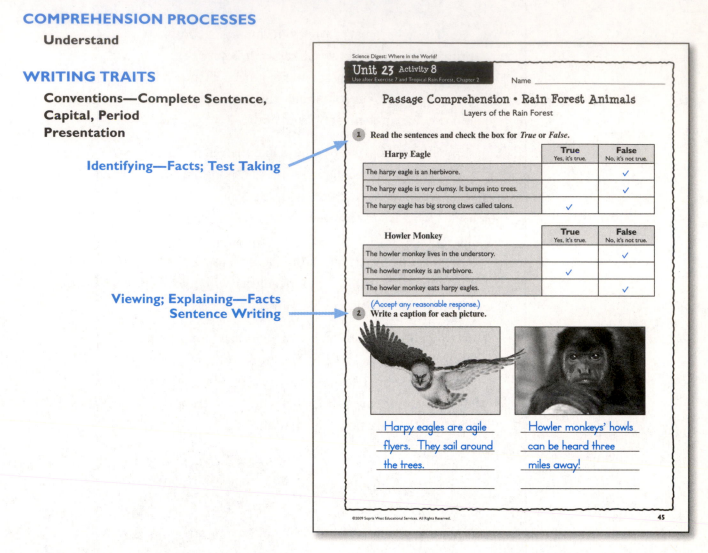

Science Digest: Where in the World!

Unit 23 Activity 8
Use after Exercise 7 and Tropical Rain Forest, Chapter 2

Name _____

Passage Comprehension • Rain Forest Animals
Layers of the Rain Forest

1. Read the sentences and check the box for *True* or *False*.

Harpy Eagle	True Yes, it's true.	False No, it's not true.
The harpy eagle is an herbivore.		✓
The harpy eagle is very clumsy. It bumps into trees.		✓
The harpy eagle has big strong claws called talons.	✓	

Howler Monkey	True Yes, it's true.	False No, it's not true.
The howler monkey lives in the understory.		✓
The howler monkey is an herbivore.	✓	
The howler monkey eats harpy eagles.		✓

(Accept any reasonable response.)
2. Write a caption for each picture.

Harpy eagles are agile flyers. They sail around the trees.

Howler monkeys' howls can be heard three miles away!

45

PROCEDURES
For each step, demonstrate and guide practice, as needed. Then have students complete the page independently.

1. **True/False: Selection Response** (Item 1)
   Have students read each sentence, determine whether the sentence is true or false, then check the correct box.

2. **Caption Writing—Specific Instructions** (Item 2)
   Have students look at the pictures and write a caption for each. Remind them to start sentences with a capital and end with a period.

ENTRY 4

COMPREHENSION PROCESSES

Understand, Create, Evaluate

WRITING TRAITS

Ideas and Content

Organization— Topic Sentence, Supporting Details

Conventions— Complete Sentence, Capital, Period

Presentation

Responding, Generating Ideas, Sentence Writing, Illustrating

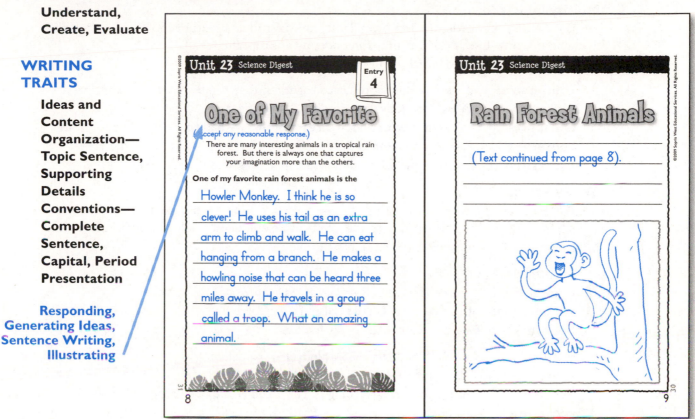

Unit 23 Science Digest

One of My Favorite

(Accept any reasonable response.)

There are many interesting animals in a tropical rain forest. But there is always one that captures your imagination more than the others.

One of my favorite rain forest animals is the

Howler Monkey. I think he is so clever! He uses his tail as an extra arm to climb and walk. He can eat hanging from a branch. He makes a howling noise that can be heard three miles away. He travels in a group called a troop. What an amazing animal.

8

Unit 23 Science Digest

Rain Forest Animals

(Text continued from page 8).

9

PROCEDURES

For each step, demonstrate and guide practice, as needed. Then have students complete the page independently.

Personal Response: Creative Writing, Illustrating—Specific Instructions

• Have students choose their favorite rain forest animal and write a paragraph explaining why it's their favorite. Remind them to start sentences with a capital and end with a period.

• Have students draw a picture of the animal they chose.

❶ SOUND REVIEW

❷ ACCURACY AND FLUENCY BUILDING

C1. Multisyllabic Words

- For the list of words divided by syllables, have students read each syllable, then the whole word. Use the word in a sentence, as appropriate.
- For the list of whole words, build accuracy and then fluency.

compost	If we mix our food scraps together, they can become . . . *compost.*
fantastic	Wow! You kids are wonderful, amazing, and . . . *fantastic.*
conserve	When it didn't rain for three months, we had to . . . *conserve* . . . water.
container	Please put water in this . . . *container.*
eventful	A lot happened on the class trip. It was very . . . *eventful.*

E1. Tricky Words

- For each Tricky Word, have students use the sounds and word parts they know to silently sound out the word. Use the word in a sentence to help with pronunciation.
- If the word is unfamiliar, tell students the word.

resources

Look at the first word. The word is *resources.* Say the word. (resources)

It's important not to use up all Earth's natural . . . *resources.*

Read the word two times. (resources, resources)

natural	I don't think Mandy's purple hair is . . . *natural.*
issue	Did you read the latest *Crazy Crafts* . . . *issue?*
grocery	Mom and Trish are going to get bread at the . . . *grocery* . . . store.
recycling	Let's help take care of the Earth by . . . *recycling.*

- Have students go back and read the whole words in the column.

❸ WORDS IN CONTEXT

★❹ FOREIGN WORDS

- Tell students they will be reading words in different languages.
- For each word, have students point to the word as is it pronounced. Model how to say the word. Say something like:

Look at the first word. That's how you say *good bye* in Spanish.

Now look at the way the word is pronounced. Listen to me say it: ah-dee-ose.

Now you say the word. (adiós)

- Have students read the translation. (Adiós means goodbye in Spanish.)

❺ MORPHOGRAPHS AND AFFIXES

- For Row A, say something like:

Read the first word. (use) Look at the next word. Read the underlined part. (re)

Now read the whole word. (reuse) When you reuse something, you use it . . . *again.*

Look at the next word. Read the underlined part. (able) Now read the whole word. (reusable)

Reusable means able to be used again.

- For Row B, have students read the underlined part, then the word.
- Repeat practice with whole words, building accuracy, then fluency.

★ = New in this unit

6 GENERALIZATION: READING NEW WORDS IN PARAGRAPHS

- Have students read the paragraph silently, then out loud. Tell students to use the sounds and word parts they know to read any difficult words.
- Repeat practice, as needed.

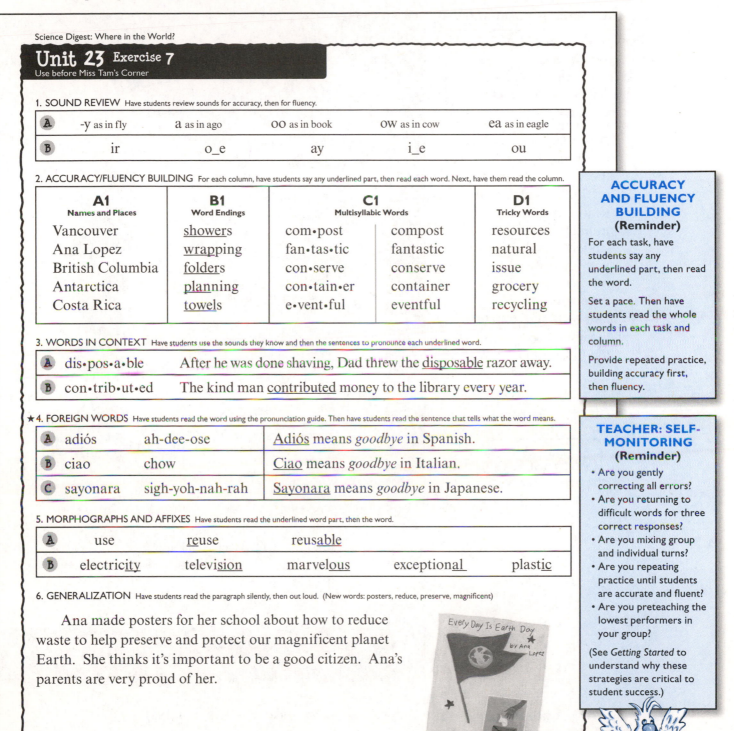

Science Digest: Where in the World?

Unit 23 Exercise 7
Use before Miss Tam's Corner

1. SOUND REVIEW Have students review sounds for accuracy, then for fluency.

A	-y as in fly	a as in ago	oo as in book	ow as in cow	ea as in eagle
B	ir	o_e	ay	i_e	ou

2. ACCURACY/FLUENCY BUILDING For each column, have students say any underlined part, then read each word. Next, have them read the column.

A1 Names and Places	B1 Word Endings	C1 Multisyllabic Words		D1 Tricky Words
Vancouver	showers	com·post	compost	resources
Ana Lopez	wrapping	fan·tas·tic	fantastic	natural
British Columbia	folders	con·serve	conserve	issue
Antarctica	planning	con·tain·er	container	grocery
Costa Rica	towels	e·vent·ful	eventful	recycling

3. WORDS IN CONTEXT Have students use the sounds they know and then the sentences to pronounce each underlined word.

A	dis·pos·a·ble	After he was done shaving, Dad threw the disposable razor away.
B	con·trib·ut·ed	The kind man contributed money to the library every year.

★4. FOREIGN WORDS Have students read the word using the pronunciation guide. Then have students read the sentence that tells what the word means.

A	adiós	ah-dee-ose	Adiós means *goodbye* in Spanish.
B	ciao	chow	Ciao means *goodbye* in Italian.
C	sayonara	sigh-yoh-nah-rah	Sayonara means *goodbye* in Japanese.

5. MORPHOGRAPHS AND AFFIXES Have students read the underlined word part, then the word.

A	use	reuse	reusable		
B	electricity	television	marvelous	exceptional	plastic

6. GENERALIZATION Have students read the paragraph silently, then out loud. (New words: posters, reduce, preserve, magnificent)

Ana made posters for her school about how to reduce waste to help preserve and protect our magnificent planet Earth. She thinks it's important to be a good citizen. Ana's parents are very proud of her.

Every Day Is Earth Day
by Ana Lopez
Reduce Litter! Keep our Earth Exceptional!

> **ACCURACY AND FLUENCY BUILDING (Reminder)**
>
> For each task, have students say any underlined part, then read the word.
>
> Set a pace. Then have students read the whole words in each task and column.
>
> Provide repeated practice, building accuracy first, then fluency.

> **TEACHER: SELF-MONITORING (Reminder)**
>
> - Are you gently correcting all errors?
> - Are you returning to difficult words for three correct responses?
> - Are you mixing group and individual turns?
> - Are you repeating practice until students are accurate and fluent?
> - Are you preteaching the lowest performers in your group?
>
> (See *Getting Started* to understand why these strategies are critical to student success.)

COMPREHENSION PROCESSES

Understand, Apply

PROCEDURES

1. Introducing Vocabulary

> ★ conserve ★ reduce,
> recycle ★ reuse
> ★ composting
> ★ exceptional, protect
> ★ marvelous

- For each vocabulary word, have students read the word by parts, then read the whole word.
- Read the student-friendly explanations to students as they follow with their fingers. Then have students use the vocabulary word by following the gray text.
- Review and discuss the illustrations.

USING VOCABULARY

WITH THE TEACHER

VOCABULARY POWER! 5

★ con·serve

Conserve means to use less of something.

One way I *conserve* energy is to turn lights off. What's another way to save energy? Use your vocabulary word.[1]

★ re·duce

Reduce means to use less of something.

To *reduce* our use of paper towels, we use cloth towels instead. How many paper towels do we use now?[2]

re·cy·cle

Recycle means to use something again, usually after it has been made into something else. Used paper is recycled into new paper.

We *recycle* the newspaper by shredding it for the rabbit cage. When we recycle pop cans, what do you think happens to them?[3]

★ re·use

Reuse means to use something again.

When you take the same homework folder home every day, you *reuse* the folder.

What else do you reuse? Use your new vocabulary word.[4]

★ = New

70

---

❶ **Apply:** Using Vocabulary—conserve (Another way to conserve energy is to dress warmly and turn down the heat.)

❷ **Apply:** Using Vocabulary—reduce (We use fewer paper towels. We use no paper towels.)

❸ **Apply:** Using Vocabulary—recycle (When we recycle pop cans, they get made into something else, maybe new pop cans.)

❹ **Apply:** Using Vocabulary—reuse (I reuse my lunchbox.)

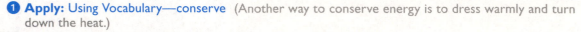

120   ★ = New in this unit

2. Now You Try It!

- Read or paraphrase the directions.
- Have students read the words by parts, then read the whole word.
- Have students explain or define the words in their own words. Say something like:

  Look at the first word. Say the parts, then read the whole word.

  (ex•cep•tion•al, exceptional)

  Now let's pretend that we're going to explain or define the word *exceptional* to a friend. [Marie], what would you say?

  Start with "Something is *exceptional* when . . ."

  (Something is exceptional when it is so good there is nothing else like it.)

  That's right.

- Have students turn to the appropriate page in the glossary and discuss how their definitions are the same as or different from the glossary's. Your students may like their definitions better.

Note: By defining a word in their own words, students are demonstrating depth of word knowledge. Verbatim responses only demonstrate memorization. Encourage paraphrasing.

MISS TAM'S CORNER

★ **com·post·ing**

Composting is saving dead plants so they decay. The decayed plants can be mixed into soil to make the soil rich.

My mother likes *composting* because it's good for the environment. She puts potato peelings, lawn clippings, and coffee grounds into a pile near her garden. What is my mother doing? **1**

Now You Try It!
Try defining the next words. Then look up the words in the glossary. Your definition might be better!

★ **ex·cep·tion·al**

Start with "Something is *exceptional* when . . ." **2**
Let's find the word on page 83.

pro·tect

Start with "*Protect* means to . . ." **3**
Let's find the word on page 84.

★ **mar·vel·ous**

Start with "*Marvelous* is another word for . . ." **4**
Let's find the word on page 84.

71

USING VOCABULARY

---

1 Apply: Using Vocabulary—composting (Your mother is composting.)

2 Understand: Defining and Using Vocabulary—exceptional; Using Glossary (Something is exceptional when it is so good there is nothing else like it.)

3 Understand: Defining and Using Vocabulary—protect; Using Glossary (Protect means to keep safe.)

4 Understand: Defining and Using Vocabulary—marvelous; Using Glossary (Marvelous is another word for wonderful and fantastic.)

STORY READING 7 INSTRUCTIONS
Students read "Miss Tam's Corner" with the teacher.

COMPREHENSION PROCESSES
Remember, Understand, Apply

PROCEDURES

1. Introducing "Miss Tam's Corner"

Identifying—Title, What; Using Vocabulary—amazing, perfect
Have students turn to page 72. Say something like:

What's the title of this article? (Miss Tam's Corner)

Like Roland, Miss Tam is very interested in protecting the Earth.

Read Miss Tam's note to you at the top of page 72. (Now that you've read this . . .)

Words that describe someone or something are called adjectives.

What are all these words? (adjectives)

Let's read all the words that Miss Tam says describe the world.
(amazing, awesome, dazzling . . .)

Now read the last part of her note. (. . . perfect. Wouldn't you agree? Earth is so . . .)

Would you all agree that Earth is perfect?

2. First Reading
- Ask questions and discuss the story as indicated by the gray text.
- Mix group and individual turns, independent of your voice.
  Have students work toward a group accuracy goal of 0–4 errors.
- After reading the story, practice any difficult words.
  Reread the story if students have not reached the accuracy goal.

3. Partner or Whisper Reading: Repeated Reading

- Have students take turns reading every other page with a partner or have students whisper read on their own.
- Continue having students track each word with their fingers.
- Have students ask themselves or their partners the gray text questions.

4. Comprehension and Skill Work
Tell students they will do Comprehension and Skill Activity 9 and Science Digest Entries 5a and 5b after they read "Miss Tam's Corner." For teacher directions, see pages 129 and 130.

5. Homework 7: Repeated Reading

WITH THE TEACHER

Miss Tam's Corner

Now that you've read this issue of the *Science Digest*, you can understand why I think our home, the Earth we share, is . . .

amazing
awesome
dazzling
* EXCEPTIONAL

fabulous
FANTASTIC
incredible
marvelous
SPLENDID

. . . perfect. Wouldn't you agree? Earth is so fine, I'm sure you would like to help protect our planet. Read on for tips on how to take care of Earth.

Why do you think Miss Tam thinks Earth is so wonderful? 1

72

73

1 Apply: Inferring; Explaining; Using Vocabulary—wonderful, splendid, marvelous (Miss Tam thinks the Earth is wonderful because she has visited many splendid places and met many marvelous people . . .)

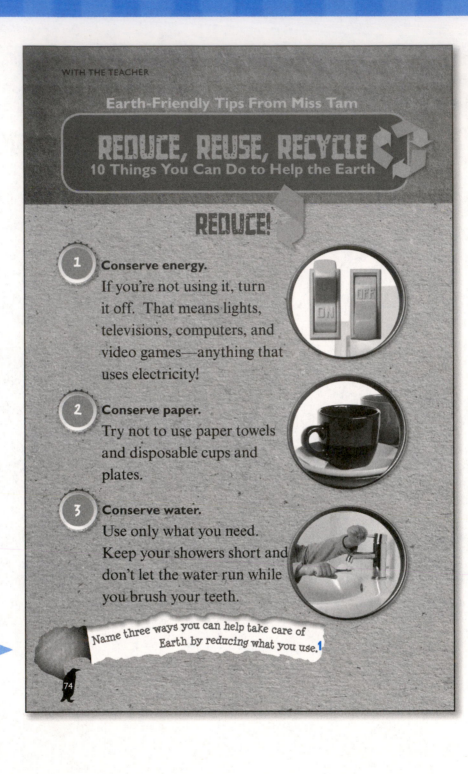

WITH THE TEACHER

Earth-Friendly Tips From Miss Tam

REDUCE, REUSE, RECYCLE
10 Things You Can Do to Help the Earth

REDUCE!

1 Conserve energy.
If you're not using it, turn it off. That means lights, televisions, computers, and video games—anything that uses electricity!

2 Conserve paper.
Try not to use paper towels and disposable cups and plates.

3 Conserve water.
Use only what you need. Keep your showers short and don't let the water run while you brush your teeth.

Name three ways you can help take care of Earth by *reducing* what you use.**1**

74

COMPREHENDING AS YOU GO

❶ **Understand:** Summarizing; Using Vocabulary—*reduce, energy* (You can reduce your use of energy by turning off lights and televisions when you're not using them. You can reduce your use of paper. You can use less water by taking short showers and not running the water while you brush your teeth.)

① **Apply:** Inferring; Explaining; Using Vocabulary—recycle (Her class is studying recycling and how to take care of the Earth.)

COMPREHENDING AS YOU GO

REUSE!

4 Write on both sides of the paper.

5 Reuse folders and notebooks.

6 Take your lunch to school in a reusable bag or plastic container.

7 Bring your own bag or backpack to the grocery store instead of using a plastic or paper bag.

Name three ways you can help take care of Earth by reusing what you use. 1

76

Poster contributed by Ben Wright, the Bronx, New York

Our Planet Earth Is Amazing by Ben F.T.E.Wright

REUSE   REUSE

Reusing helps preserve our natural resources.

77

❶ **Understand:** Summarizing; Using Vocabulary—reuse (You can write on both sides of paper. You can take lunch to school in a bag or lunch box that you can use again. You can take your own reusable bags to the store for carrying groceries.)

WITH THE TEACHER

RECYCLE!

8 **Set up recycle bins at home.** Make it a habit to recycle newspapers, cans, plastic, and glass.

9 **Make your own wrapping paper using old calendar pictures or old drawings.**

10 **Create a composting bin with your parents' help.** Food scraps can go in the bin instead of into the trash. The scraps will turn into rich soil for the garden.

Name three ways you can help take care of Earth by recycling what you use. 1

78

MISS TAM'S CORNER

Poster contributed by Maya Martinez, the Bronx, New York

Magnificent and Marvelous Earth and Me by Maya Martinez

It's Not Yucky! It's Just Ducky!

Reduce Waste by Composting!

79

1 **Understand:** Summarizing; Using Vocabulary—recycle, composting (You recycle your cans, plastic, and glass at home. You can make your own wrapping paper with old comics and calendar pages. You can set up a composting bin for your food scraps.)

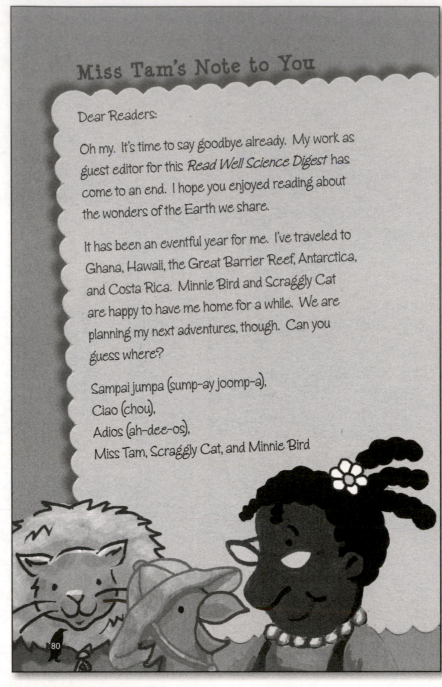

Miss Tam's Note to You

Dear Readers:

Oh my. It's time to say goodbye already. My work as guest editor for this *Read Well Science Digest* has come to an end. I hope you enjoyed reading about the wonders of the Earth we share.

It has been an eventful year for me. I've traveled to Ghana, Hawaii, the Great Barrier Reef, Antarctica, and Costa Rica. Minnie Bird and Scraggly Cat are happy to have me home for a while. We are planning my next adventures, though. Can you guess where?

Sampai jumpa (sump-ay joomp-a),
Ciao (chou),
Adios (ah-dee-os),
Miss Tam, Scraggly Cat, and Minnie Bird

After Reading Page 80

1 Remember: Identifying—What
What is Miss Tam planning?
(She is planning her next adventure.)

2 Apply: Inferring
Miss Tam said good bye in Italian and Spanish. Sampai jumpa (sump-ay joomp-a) is Indonesian. What do you think it means? (good bye)
Where do you think Miss Tam will go next?
(Japan, Italy, Spain, Mexico . . .)

You'll never know where Miss Tam might show up. She might show up in your backyard. I wonder where in the world Miss Tam will go next.

CROSSWORD PUZZLE

COMPREHENSION PROCESSES

Remember, Understand

Identifying—What
Using Vocabulary—marvelous, reduce, exceptional, reuse, conserve, recycle

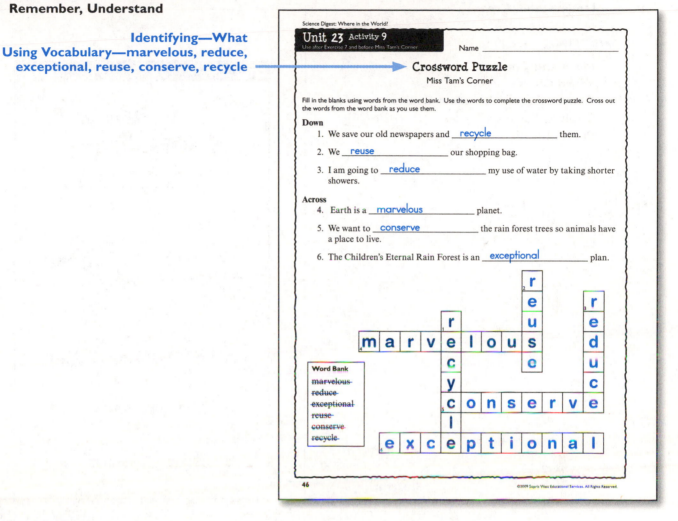

Science Digest: Where in the World?

Unit 23 Activity 9
Use after Exercise 7 and before Miss Tam's Corner

Name _____

Crossword Puzzle
Miss Tam's Corner

Fill in the blanks using words from the word bank. Use the words to complete the crossword puzzle. Cross out the words from the word bank as you use them.

Down

1. We save our old newspapers and ___recycle___ them.

2. We ___reuse___ our shopping bag.

3. I am going to ___reduce___ my use of water by taking shorter showers.

Across

4. Earth is a ___marvelous___ planet.

5. We want to ___conserve___ the rain forest trees so animals have a place to live.

6. The Children's Eternal Rain Forest is an ___exceptional___ plan.

Word Bank
~~marvelous~~
~~reduce~~
~~exceptional~~
~~reuse~~
~~conserve~~
~~recycle~~

46

©2009 Sopris West Educational Services. All Rights Reserved.

PROCEDURES

For each step, demonstrate and guide practice, as needed. Then have students complete the page independently.

Vocabulary: Sentence Completion—Basic Instructions

• Have students read the words in the Word Bank. Then have students read the sentences and fill in the blanks with words from the Word Bank.

• Have students trace the words in the crossword puzzle.

ENTRIES 5a, 5b

COMPREHENSION PROCESSES
Understand, Create

WRITING TRAITS
Ideas and Content
Word Choice
Conventions—Complete Sentence,
Capital, Period
Presentation

Illustrating

PROCEDURES

For each step, demonstrate and guide practice, as needed. Then have students complete the page independently.

1. **Cover: Illustrating—Specific Instructions** (Entry 5a)

   Have students draw a picture to illustrate the cover of their Science Digest. Have students select a subject that captivated their interest. Say something like:

   Think about this edition of the Science Digest. What did you think was the most fascinating part? Was it the cold frozen land of Antarctica? The penguins? Or perhaps the rain forest? Or a rain forest animal? Draw something that you found really fascinating, awesome, amazing, and exceptional!

2. **Personal Response: Creative Writing—Specific Instructions** (Entry 5b)

   Have students choose somewhere on Earth they would like to visit and write a sentence or two telling why. Remind students to start sentences with a capital and end with a period.

ENTRIES 5a, 5b *(continued)*

Generating Ideas, Sentence Writing

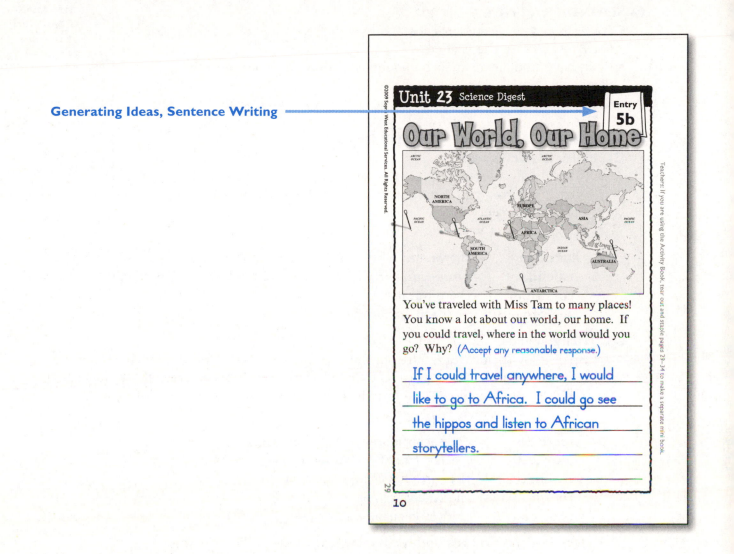

❶ SOUND REVIEW

❷ SOUND PRACTICE

- For each task, have students spell and say the focus sound in the gray bar. For Bossy E̲, read the header.
- Next, have students read each underlined sound, the word, then the whole column.
- Repeat with each column, building accuracy first, then fluency.

❸ ACCURACY AND FLUENCY BUILDING

C1. Multisyllabic Words

- For the list of words divided by syllables, have students read each syllable, then the whole word. Use the word in a sentence, as appropriate.
- For the list of whole words, build accuracy and then fluency.

attract	The woman tried to blend in. She didn't want to . . . *attract* . . . attention.
calendar	I wanted to know which day the 12th fell on, so I looked at the . . . *calendar*.
container	There was milk in the . . . *container*.
secretive	My friend was being very . . . *secretive*.

D1. Tricky Words

- For each Tricky Word, have students use the sounds and word parts they know to silently sound out the word. Use the word in a sentence to help with pronunciation.
- If the word is unfamiliar, tell students the word.

species	Humpback whales are a . . . *species*.
territory	Many animals are protective of their . . . *territory*.
journey	I packed lots of clothes for my long . . . *journey*.
resources	The Earth has limited . . . *resources*.
rough	The sandpaper was really . . . *rough*.
precious	Jose's little puppy is absolutely . . . *precious*.

- Have students go back and read the whole words in the column.

❹ WORD ENDINGS

Have students read the underlined word, then the word with an ending. Use the words in sentences, as needed.

★❺ MONTHS OF THE YEAR

- Tell students they will be reading the months in a year.
- Have students read each word.

❻ MORPHOGRAPHS AND AFFIXES

- Have students read the underlined part, then the whole word. Use words in sentences, as needed.
- Repeat practice with whole words, mixing group and individual turns. Build accuracy, then fluency.

> **ACCURACY AND FLUENCY BUILDING (Reminder)**
>
> For each task, have students say any underlined part, then read the word.
>
> Set a pace. Then have students read the whole words in each task and column.
>
> Provide repeated practice, building accuracy first, then fluency.

★ = New in this unit

Fluency

Unit 23 Exercise 8
Use before Grade 3

1. SOUND REVIEW Use selected Sound Cards from Units 1–19.

2. SOUND PRACTICE In each column, have students spell and say the sound, next say any underlined sound and the word, then read the column.

ow as in cow	**-y** as in baby	**e** as in Ed	Bossy **E**
t<u>ow</u>els	chill<u>y</u>	d<u>e</u>pths	sh<u>a</u>de
h<u>ow</u>ls	empt<u>y</u>	tr<u>e</u>k	v<u>i</u>nes
pr<u>ow</u>ls	fanc<u>y</u>	ch<u>e</u>st	h<u>u</u>ge

3. ACCURACY/FLUENCY BUILDING For each column, have students say any underlined part, then read each word. Next, have them read the column.

A1 Mixed Practice	**B1** Compound Words	**C1** Multisyllabic Words		**D1** Tricky Words
br<u>ea</u>th	<u>farewell</u>	at•tract	attract	species
br<u>ea</u>the	birthdays	cal•en•dar	calendar	territory
freeze	eyesight	con•tain•er	container	journey
agile	underwater	se•cre•tive	secretive	resources
m<u>o</u>lt				rough
jag<u>uar</u>				precious

4. WORD ENDINGS Have students read each underlined word, then the word with an ending.

<u>speckl</u>ed	<u>march</u>ing	<u>recogniz</u>ed	<u>predator</u>s
<u>perch</u>ed	<u>acre</u>s	<u>parade</u>s	<u>degree</u>s

★5. MONTHS OF THE YEAR Have students read the words.

Ⓐ	January	February	March	April	May	June
Ⓑ	July	August	September	October	November	December

6. MORPHOGRAPHS AND AFFIXES Have students read the underlined word part, then the word.

Ⓐ	marve<u>lous</u>	expedi<u>tion</u>	uncomfort<u>able</u>	responsibili<u>ty</u>
Ⓑ	environ<u>ment</u>	<u>un</u>protected	<u>in</u>stinct	accomplish<u>ment</u>

FLUENCY PASSAGE INSTRUCTIONS

This Story Reading targets fluency as the primary goal of instruction and practice. Students do repeated readings of this passage to improve accuracy, expression, and rate.

Note: The fluency passage is found in *Exercise Book 4* on pages 34–35.

PROCEDURES

1. **Warm-Up: Partner Reading or Whisper Reading**

   Before beginning group Story Reading, have students finger track and partner or whisper read the selection.

2. **First Reading**

   • Mix group and individual turns, independent of your voice. Have students work toward a group accuracy goal of 0–6 errors. Quietly keep track of errors made by all students in the group.

   • After reading the story, practice any difficult words. Reread the story if students have not reached the accuracy goal.

3. **Second Reading, Short Passage Practice: Developing Prosody**

   • Demonstrate reading the first stanza with expression and fluency. Have students finger track as you read.

   • Have students choral read the first stanza. Encourage reading with expression and fluency.

   • Repeat with second stanza.

4. **Third Reading, Group Timed Readings: Repeated Reading**

    • Select a page. Encourage each child to work for a personal best. Have students whisper read for a one-minute Timed Reading. Tell students to go back to the top of the page and keep reading until the minute is up.

   • Have students put their finger on the last word they read and count the number of words read correctly in one minute.

   • Have students do a Second Timed Reading of the same page.

   • Have students try to beat their last score.

   • Celebrate improvements.

5. **Written Assessment (Comprehension and Skill)**

   Tell students they will do a Written Assessment after they read "Grade 3." For teacher directions, see pages 137–139.

6. **Homework 8: Repeated Reading**

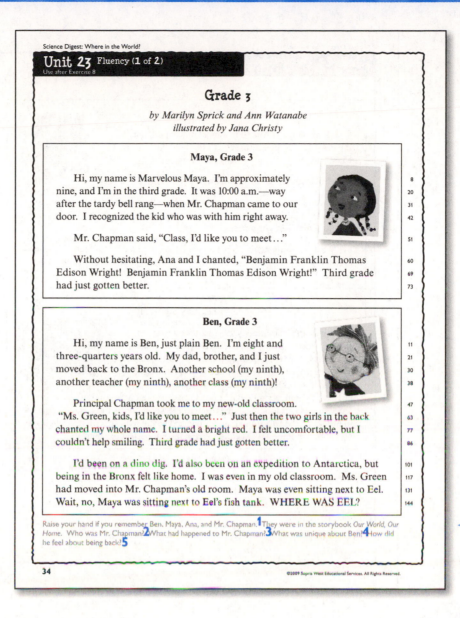

Science Digest: Where in the World?

Unit 23 Fluency (1 of 2)
Use after Exercise 8

Grade 3

by Marilyn Sprick and Ann Watanabe
illustrated by Jana Christy

Maya, Grade 3

Hi, my name is Marvelous Maya. I'm approximately nine, and I'm in the third grade. It was 10:00 a.m.—way after the tardy bell rang—when Mr. Chapman came to our door. I recognized the kid who was with him right away.

Mr. Chapman said, "Class, I'd like you to meet…"

Without hesitating, Ana and I chanted, "Benjamin Franklin Thomas Edison Wright! Benjamin Franklin Thomas Edison Wright!" Third grade had just gotten better.

Ben, Grade 3

Hi, my name is Ben, just plain Ben. I'm eight and three-quarters years old. My dad, brother, and I just moved back to the Bronx. Another school (my ninth), another teacher (my ninth), another class (my ninth)!

Principal Chapman took me to my new-old classroom. "Ms. Green, kids, I'd like you to meet…" Just then the two girls in the back chanted my whole name. I turned a bright red. I felt uncomfortable, but I couldn't help smiling. Third grade had just gotten better.

I'd been on a dino dig. I'd also been on an expedition to Antarctica, but being in the Bronx felt like home. I was even in my old classroom. Ms. Green had moved into Mr. Chapman's old room. Maya was even sitting next to Eel. Wait, no, Maya was sitting next to Eel's fish tank. WHERE WAS EEL?

Raise your hand if you remember Ben, Maya, Ana, and Mr. Chapman.¹ They were in the storybook *Our World, Our Home.* Who was Mr. Chapman?² What had happened to Mr. Chapman?³ What was unique about Ben?⁴ How did he feel about being back?⁵

34   ©2009 Sopris West Educational Services. All Rights Reserved.

COMPREHENDING AS YOU GO

❶ **Apply:** Making Connections
❷ **Understand:** Identifying—Who (Mr. Chapman was Maya's second grade teacher.)
❸ **Understand:** Explaining (Mr. Chapman is the school principal now.)
❹ **Understand:** Explaining—Character Traits (Characterization); Using Vocabulary—unique (Ben was named after three famous scientists. He's traveled all over the world . . .)
❺ **Apply:** Inferring; Explaining (Ben is happy to be back. He said the Bronx felt like home.)

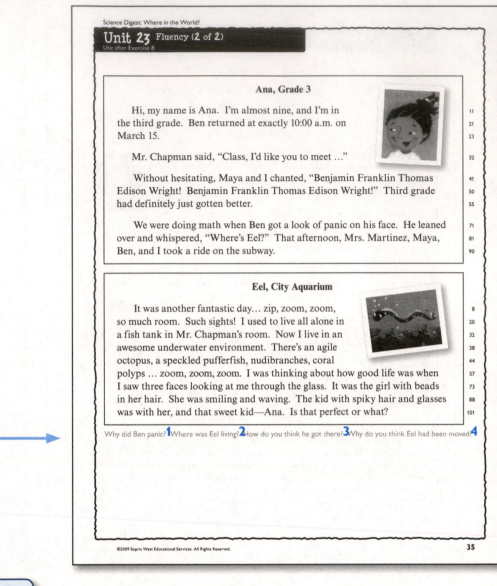

Science Digest: Where in the World?

Unit 23 Fluency (2 of 2)
Use after Exercise 8

Ana, Grade 3

Hi, my name is Ana. I'm almost nine, and I'm in the third grade. Ben returned at exactly 10:00 a.m. on March 15.

Mr. Chapman said, "Class, I'd like you to meet ..."

Without hesitating, Maya and I chanted, "Benjamin Franklin Thomas Edison Wright! Benjamin Franklin Thomas Edison Wright!" Third grade had definitely just gotten better.

We were doing math when Ben got a look of panic on his face. He leaned over and whispered, "Where's Eel?" That afternoon, Mrs. Martinez, Maya, Ben, and I took a ride on the subway.

Eel, City Aquarium

It was another fantastic day... zip, zoom, zoom, so much room. Such sights! I used to live all alone in a fish tank in Mr. Chapman's room. Now I live in an awesome underwater environment. There's an agile octopus, a speckled pufferfish, nudibranches, coral polyps ... zoom, zoom, zoom. I was thinking about how good life was when I saw three faces looking at me through the glass. It was the girl with beads in her hair. She was smiling and waving. The kid with spiky hair and glasses was with her, and that sweet kid—Ana. Is that perfect or what?

Why did Ben panic? ❶ Where was Eel living? ❷ How do you think he got there? ❸ Why do you think Eel had been moved? ❹

35

COMPREHENDING AS YOU GO

❶ **Apply:** Inferring, Explaining (Ben panicked because Eel wasn't in the aquarium.)

❷ **Apply:** Inferring, Explaining (Eel was living in the city aquarium.)

❸ **Analyze:** Drawing Conclusions (Mr. Chapman brought him to the aquarium . . .)

❹ **Analyze:** Drawing Conclusions (Eel grew too big for the fish tank. The new teacher didn't like the eel . . .)

WRITTEN ASSESSMENT (1 of 3)

COMPREHENSION PROCESSES
Remember, Understand, Apply

WRITING TRAITS
Ideas and Content
Word Choice
Conventions—Complete Sentence, Capital, Period
Presentation

Test Taking

Unit **23** Written Assessment
Use after Exercise 8 and Grade 3

WARM-UP

| scientists | blizzard | solve | Antarctica | emperor |

Antarctica Through the Winter

Antarctica is the coldest place on Earth. It is frozen all year. On a winter's day, it may be 100 degrees below zero. It is also the windiest place on Earth. Winds race across the ice at 200 miles per hour.

Most animals leave for the winter. Only emperor penguins stay. What about people? Some scientists stay through the winter. People who help them also stay. About a thousand people live in Antarctica through the winter.

Winters in Antarctica are hard. Of course, it is freezing. It is also dark. People must wear layers of clothing. They must have the right tools. They must be careful not to get caught in a blizzard.

Once winter arrives, people cannot come and go. Planes can't land. Ships can't cross the ice. There are no stores. When people stay for the winter, they must have everything they need.

Why do people stay? Scientists study the land. They study the ice. They study the air. They learn about the ocean and food chains.

Scientists are doing important work. By studying Antarctica, they are learning how Earth is changing. Scientists are learning how to solve problems. They are learning information that will help keep Earth healthy.

continued

102 ©2009 Sopris West Educational Services. All Rights Reserved.

137

WRITTEN ASSESSMENT (2 of 3)

Using Graphic Organizer (Hierarchy Chart); Explaining—Supporting Details; Sentence Writing

Using Graphic Organizer (Matrix) Distinguishing—Cause/Effect Sentence Writing

Drawing Conclusions

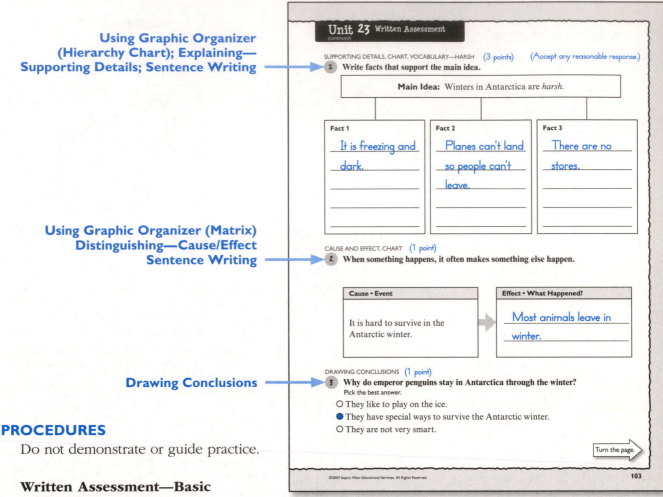

Unit 23 Written Assessment
(continued)

SUPPORTING DETAILS, CHART, VOCABULARY—HARSH   (3 points)   (Accept any reasonable response.)

1 **Write facts that support the main idea.**

Main Idea: Winters in Antarctica are *harsh*.

Fact 1	Fact 2	Fact 3
It is freezing and dark.	Planes can't land so people can't leave.	There are no stores.

CAUSE AND EFFECT, CHART   (1 point)

2 **When something happens, it often makes something else happen.**

Cause • Event	Effect • What Happened?
It is hard to survive in the Antarctic winter.	Most animals leave in winter.

DRAWING CONCLUSIONS   (1 point)

3 **Why do emperor penguins stay in Antarctica through the winter?**
Pick the best answer.
○ They like to play on the ice.
● They have special ways to survive the Antarctic winter.
○ They are not very smart.

Turn the page.

©2009 Sopris West Educational Services. All Rights Reserved.   103

PROCEDURES

Do not demonstrate or guide practice.

Written Assessment—Basic Instructions

1. Introduce the Written Assessment.
    - Tell students that their work today is an opportunity for them to show what they can do independently. Say something like:
      You should be very proud of your accomplishments. Remember, on a Written Assessment, you get to show me what you can do all by yourself.

    - Tell students they will whisper read the passage and then answer the questions without help.

2. Check for student understanding.
    Say something like:
    Look at your assessment. What are you going to do first? (write my name)

    What are going to do next? (whisper read the passage)
    What will you do after you read the passage? (answer the questions)

    That's great. Now what will you do if you get to a hard question?
    (reread the question and try again)
    That's right. What should you do if it's still hard? (reread the passage and try again)
    Very good. And if you still aren't sure, what will you do? (do my best and keep going)

WRITTEN ASSESSMENT (3 of 3)

Identifying—Supporting Details, Facts

Inferring—Main Idea

**Responding, Generating Ideas
Sentence Writing**

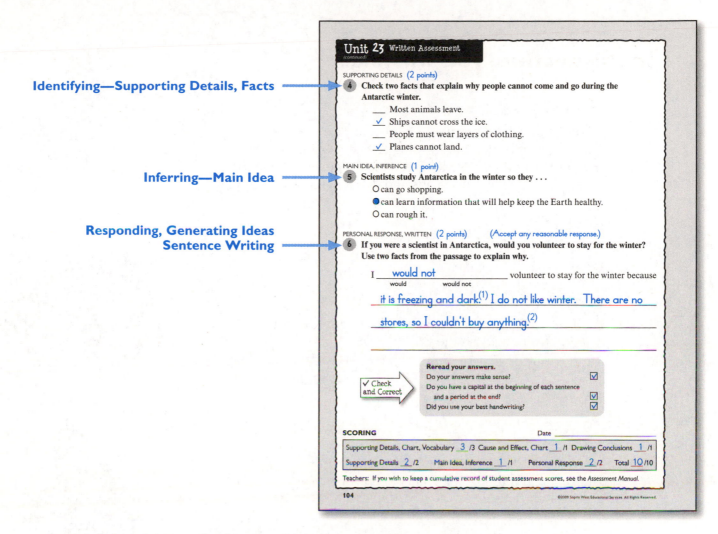

Unit 23 Written Assessment
(continued)

SUPPORTING DETAILS (2 points)

4 **Check two facts that explain why people cannot come and go during the Antarctic winter.**

____ Most animals leave.

✓ Ships cannot cross the ice.

____ People must wear layers of clothing.

✓ Planes cannot land.

MAIN IDEA, INFERENCE (1 point)

5 **Scientists study Antarctica in the winter so they . . .**

○ can go shopping.

● can learn information that will help keep the Earth healthy.

○ can rough it.

PERSONAL RESPONSE, WRITTEN (2 points) (Accept any reasonable response.)

6 **If you were a scientist in Antarctica, would you volunteer to stay for the winter? Use two facts from the passage to explain why.**

I ___would not___ volunteer to stay for the winter because
     (would   would not)

it is freezing and dark.[1] I do not like winter. There are no

stores, so I couldn't buy anything.[2]

✓ Check and Correct

Reread your answers.

Do your answers make sense? ☑

Do you have a capital at the beginning of each sentence and a period at the end? ☑

Did you use your best handwriting? ☑

SCORING   Date _____

| Supporting Details, Chart, Vocabulary | 3 /3 | Cause and Effect, Chart | 1 /1 | Drawing Conclusions | 1 /1 |
| Supporting Details | 2 /2 | Main Idea, Inference | 1 /1 | Personal Response | 2 /2 | Total 10 /10 |

Teachers: If you wish to keep a cumulative record of student assessment scores, see the Assessment Manual.

104   ©2009 Sopris West Educational Services. All Rights Reserved.

3. Remind students to check and correct.
    When you finish your assessment, what should you do? (check and correct)
    That's right. Go to the top of the page. Reread the questions and make sure your answers make sense. Fix anything that doesn't sound right. Make sure you have an answer for every question.

4. Remind students what to do when they finish their work.

End of the Unit

In this section, you will find:

Making Decisions

As you near the end of the unit, plan to give the Written Assessment and the Oral Reading Fluency Assessment to each child in your group. Use this section as a general guide for making instructional decisions and doing diagnostic planning.

Written Assessment

The Unit 23 Written Assessment is located on page 101 of *Activity Book 4* and on the CD.

Oral Reading Fluency Assessment

The Unit 23 Oral Reading Fluency Assessment is located on page 144 and in the *Assessment Manual*.

Certificate of Achievement

Celebrate your children's accomplishments. When your students master the unit skills, send home the Certificate of Achievement.

Making Decisions

GENERAL ASSESSMENT GUIDELINES

1. After students read Story Reading 8, "Grade 3," give the group the Unit 23 Written Assessment in place of Comprehension and Skill Work. Follow the instructions on pages 137–139 of this guide.

2. While the group is completing the Written Assessment, or any time during the day, administer the Oral Reading Fluency Assessment. Assess each student individually.

   Optional: Graph the results of the assessment. (See Unit 21 Teacher's Guide, pages 100 and 103.)
   - If the student's words correct per minute go up, congratulate the student.
   - If the student's words correct per minute go down, discuss the student's overall improvement and help him or her identify ways to improve for the next assessment.

3. Score oral fluency responses on the Student Assessment Record. Adhere to the scoring criteria in the *Assessment Manual*. Use a stopwatch to time how long it takes each student to read the Oral Reading Fluency Passage, and record errors.

USING WRITTEN ASSESSMENT RESULTS

Results of the Written Assessment *should not* be used to determine whether a student or group of students continues forward in the program. As long as students pass the Oral Reading Fluency Assessment, they should continue forward with the next unit.

The Written Assessment should be used to informally monitor how well students read independently and answer questions in writing. If any student has difficulty with the Written Assessment, re-administer the assessment orally.

If the student has difficulty answering the questions orally:
- Record the types of errors (e.g., main idea, sequencing, open-ended response).
- Provide explicit instruction for these types of questions during reading group, before independent work, and in tutorials, as needed.
   1) Demonstrate (or model) appropriate responses, guide practice, and provide opportunities for independent practice.
   2) For inferential questions, think aloud with students—explain how you arrive at an answer.
   3) For literal questions, teach students to reread a passage, locate information, reread the question, and respond.

USING THE ORAL READING FLUENCY RESULTS

At the end of each unit, you will need to make decisions regarding student progress. Should students go forward in the program? Does the group need extra practice before proceeding? Do individuals require more assistance and practice to continue working in their group? These decisions all require use of the oral reading fluency data and professional judgment. As you analyze assessment results, watch for trends and anomalies.

See the *Assessment Manual* for detailed information and instructional recommendations. General guidelines and recommendations follow:

Strong Pass ≥ 128 WCPM 0–2 errors	• Continue with the current pace of instruction. • Have students set goals. (Until students are reading approximately 180 words correct per minute, oral reading fluency continues to be an instructional goal.)
Pass 107–127 WCPM 0–2 errors	• Continue with the current pace of instruction. Consider increasing fluency practice.
No Pass ≤ 106 WCPM	• If a child scores a No Pass but has previously passed all assessments, you may wish to advance the student to the next unit, then carefully monitor the student. • If a child scores a No Pass but has previously passed all assessments, you may wish to advance the student to the next unit and also provide additional practice opportunities. (See below.) • If a child scores two consecutive No Passes or periodic No Passes, additional practice must be provided. (See below.) • If a child scores three consecutive No Passes, the student should be placed in a lower-performing group.

RED FLAG
A No Pass is a red flag. A mild early intervention can prevent an intense and time-consuming intervention in the future.

Added Practice Options for Groups
Warm-Ups:
• Begin each lesson with Partner Reading of the previous day's homework.
• Begin each lesson with a five-minute Fluency Booster. Place copies of the Unit 15–22 *Read Well* Homework in three-ring notebooks. Each day, have students begin Finger Tracking and Whisper Reading at Unit 15, Homework 1. At the end of five minutes, have students mark where they are in their notebooks. The next day, the goal is to read farther.
• Begin each Story Reading with a review of the previous day's story.
• After reading the story, include Short Passage Practice on a daily basis.

Jell-Well Reviews: A Jell-Well Review is the *Read Well* term for a review of earlier units. A Jell-Well Review is a period of time taken to celebrate what children have learned and an opportunity to firm up their foundation of learning. To complete a Jell-Well Review, take the group back to the last unit for which all students scored Strong Passes. Then quickly cycle back up. See the *Assessment Manual* for how to build a Jell-Well Review.

Added Practice Options for Individual Students

Tutorials: Set up five-minute tutorials on a daily basis with an assistant, trained volunteer, or cross-age tutor. Have the tutor provide Short Passage Practice and Timed Readings.

Double Dose: Find ways to provide a double dose of *Read Well* instruction.
- Have the student work in his or her group *and* a lower-performing group.
- Have an instructional assistant, older student, or parent volunteer preview or review lessons.
- Have an instructional assistant provide instruction with Extra Practice lessons.
- Preview new lessons or review previous lessons.

END-OF-THE-UNIT CELEBRATION

When students pass the Oral Reading Fluency Assessment, celebrate with the Certificate of Achievement on page 145.

Note: Using the Flesch-Kincaid Grade Level readability formula, the Unit 23 Assessment has a 3.3 readability level. Readabilities are based on number of words per sentence and number of syllables per word. Adding one or two multisyllabic words can increase readability by a month or two. Though we are attending to readability for the assessments, the overriding factor is decodability.

TRICKY WORD and FOCUS SKILL WARM-UP

recognized	covered	scurried	enough	temperature	confused

ORAL READING FLUENCY PASSAGE

Toby and Flash

★Toby and Flash were just a few weeks old. Their plump   11
bodies were covered with fluffy gray feathers. They were still   21
small enough to enjoy perching on their father's feet. But they   32
were also discovering that it was fun to explore.   41

One day Toby and Flash wandered off. They roamed the   51
vast land surrounding the penguin rookery. Then Toby began to   61
feel unsettled. He looked around. "Flash, I'm confused. Where   70
are we?" he said. "I'm hungry, and freezing cold! Let's find our   82
parents."   83

Flash hesitated. The temperature was dropping. He   90
didn't want to admit it, but he was freezing too. "Ok, Toby, if   104
you insist. We'll go back." Flash turned around and began to   115
strut back to the penguin colony. Toby scurried after him.   124

Then, in the distance, two emperor penguins emerged   132
from the huddled group and bellowed. Flash and Toby   141
recognized them. They were thrilled. They ran as fast as they   152
could to their fathers.   156

ORAL READING FLUENCY	Start timing at the ★. Mark errors. Make a single slash in the text (/) at 60 seconds. If the student completes the passage in less than 60 seconds, have the student go back to the ★ and continue reading. Make a double slash (//) in the text at 60 seconds.
WCPM	Determine words correct per minute by subtracting errors from words read in 60 seconds.
STRONG PASS	The student scores no more than 2 errors on the first pass through the passage and reads 128 or more words correct per minute. Proceed to Unit 24.
PASS	The student scores no more than 2 errors on the first pass through the passage and reads 107 to 127 words correct per minute. Proceed to Unit 24.
NO PASS	The student scores 3 or more errors on the first pass through the passage and/or reads 106 or fewer words correct per minute. Provide added fluency practice. For 2 or 3 days, reteach an exercise page and use a homework passage for fluency practice, then retest.